NOT WITH MY HUSBAND, YOU DON'T

MARGARET KENT is a practicing attorney specializing in international law and divorce law in Florida. Her innovative marriage course, developed in 1969, won her national acclaim. In 1985, Ms. Kent published her marriage strategies in her first book, *How to Marry the Man of Your Choice*. The privately printed edition, which sold for $95, made her an instant sensation and a sought-after guest on such television shows as "Donahue," "Sally Jessy Raphael," "Larry King," and "The Oprah Winfrey Show."

ALSO BY THE AUTHOR:

How to Marry the Man of Your Choice
Love at Work (co-authored with Robert Feinschreiber)

Not with My Husband, You Don't

Margaret Kent

WARNER BOOKS

A Time Warner Company

*To the women who wouldn't let "the other woman"
ruin their marriages*

Warner Books, Inc., 666 Fifth Avenue, New York, NY 10103
 A Time Warner Company

Printed in the United States of America
First printing: November 1990
10 9 8 7 6 5 4 3 2 1

Library of Congress Cataloging-in-Publication Data

Kent, Margaret, 1942–
  Not with my husband, you don't / Margaret Kent.
     p.   cm.
  ISBN 0-446-39151-4
  1. Adultery. 2. Wives—Life skills guides. 3. Marriage
—Psychological aspects. I. Title.
HQ806.K46   1990
  306.73′6—dc20   90-34342
                                                          CIP

*Book design by Giorgetta Bell McRee
Cover design by Anne Twomey*

ACKNOWLEDGMENTS

Many wonderful people helped produce this book, but special thanks go to:

My husband, Robert Feinschreiber, for collaborating with me throughout the book process, and for refraining from adultery.

My father-in-law, Selven Feinschreiber, for sharing his expertise and insights.

My daughter, Kathryn Feinschreiber, for encouraging me to begin this project.

My son, Steven Feinschreiber, for encouraging me to complete this project.

My assistant, Doreen Perry, for making this book a reality.

My agent, Sandra Choron, for believing in the book from the start.

My senior editor, Susan Suffes, for dealing with us.

My publisher, Nansey Neiman, for her courage to pursue this project.

Warner Books, Inc., for its great and competent staff.

CONTENTS

PREFACE *ix*

INTRODUCTION *1*

1. IS HE CHEATING? *5*
2. PROVING HIS INFIDELITY *32*
3. THAT BASTARD *61*
4. WHAT ABOUT ME? *79*
5. THE BITCH *102*
6. FIGHTING BACK *129*
7. MANIPULATING HIS MISTRESS *166*
8. SAVING YOUR MARRIAGE *172*

CONCLUSION *193*

PREFACE

With the title, *Not with* My *Husband, You Don't*, you could be pondering, "What about your husband, Margaret? How do you know *he's* faithful? And how do you know for sure?" If you probed still further, you would be asking, "If he is committing adultery, what would *you* do about it? How could you survive it?" You would be thinking these same thoughts because they are equally relevant in your own situation. They apply, in fact, to every married woman.

Now that you've asked your questions, let me ask just one: Is your spouse adultery prone? As we will find out, some men cheat, others don't, but every husband is a potential adulterer. You can minimize the chances of adultery if you know why it happens.

If you suspect infidelity, a barrage of emotions and fears overcomes you. You'll be in shock for a while, but as you start to regain your composure, your own feelings can conflict and confuse. One day you resolve to end your marriage, the next day you vow to save it. You might even wonder if you are losing your mind completely. Perhaps you've doubted your sanity because, despite it all, you want him back. Your good sense tells you to fight for him, even to confront her, if necessary. But how do you do it?

What you need is empathy. Can you really expect others to know what you feel? It's ironic that close family and friends often can't deal with your pain. You're better off talking to a sympathetic stranger—a fellow passenger on a plane, for instance, whom you never expect to see again.

You can evaluate your husband's potential to cheat and confirm your suspicions. If you discover he has wandered, you need a plan to control yourself long enough to act wisely. If you want to stay married, you need to know how to fight back. Knowledge and self-control can give you the courage to succeed. This book guides you through the difficult moments of infidelity. These are harsh strategies, but there are harsh realities. The tougher the situation, the tougher you must be. The hope is that you find the necessary tools to command your life and do what is best for you and your children.

Your husband might be faithful, but how do you know for sure? Security and peace of mind are most important over the long term. After you review the initial portion of this book, and you discover that he isn't cheating, you'll be able to put your mind to rest (with one eye open, anyway).

This book will help you make it on your own, through all the stages of a real or potentially unfaithful spouse. And you'll be making decisions based on their long-term consequences.

You might think that the techniques in this book are manipulative. They are! When you are competing against the other woman for your husband, you can be sure she's manipulating you. With these strategies, your techniques of dealing with her, whether manipulative or not, are likely to prevail. Then you can win him back.

As I traveled across the world, in conjunction with *How to Marry the Man of Your Choice*, I discovered that married women everywhere have one paramount goal: keeping their husbands faithful. Whether I met with a woman in Dublin who believed that her husband was having a relationship because "he had to" or a woman in Australia who said that her husband's view was "fidelity is obsolete," I discovered that the problems are similar and so are the techniques.

As an attorney, I have utilized the experiences of various women who have faced their husbands' adultery and survived. You have options. The key is choosing the right ones. Don't be the last to know.

MARGARET KENT

INTRODUCTION

Many women, when confronted with adultery, will take action quickly, almost as if it was a reflex. Just as she will cover her eyes when a bright light shines in them, a wife may react without thought and do something that will later cause regret. As an attorney, I have seen women file for divorce at the mere suspicion their husbands were unfaithful.

You might think your husband has been cheating, but you don't know for sure. In many cases, a husband may leave his wife for someone else, and the wife never knows why he left. Some women think that their husbands are cheating, but they aren't. This book is designed to help women determine the truth and assuage their fears.

Is your husband faithful? If you don't know for sure, take this simple test:

1. Does he work late all the time?
2. Does he disappear for hours on weekends?
3. Has your household budget been cut down by his expenses?
4. Is he too exhausted to make love to you as often as before?
5. Is he talking less freely about himself?
6. Is he suddenly concerned about his looks?
7. Is he seeking privacy for his phone calls?
8. Is he cleaning the interior of his car more often?
9. Is he encouraging you to take trips to see relatives?
10. Is he buying you more gifts?

If you answered "yes" to even one of these questions, it's time to find out if your husband might be cheating.

If you think he is, verify your suspicions. Mistrust alone can erode relationships, so resolve any doubts. If you discover that he is unfaithful, you have to decide what you should do about it, since you have a wide range of options, from forgiving him to seeking divorce. You can choose the best for you and your children.

This book will give you further guidelines to discover if he's cheating.

If he is, the book will give you additional strategies to preserve the marriage by getting rid of the other woman and fighting for your husband.

If your spouse has cheated, assess the damage to your relationship. The greatest injury may have been to your pride. This book will show you the questions to ask yourself to determine if you want to continue your marriage.

You probably feel that no one understands your anguish, but, in truth, many women face this situation. Being human isn't always fun, but there is no need to feel embarrassed about these circumstances. You've got to use your good sense to do what's best for you. This book will help to bring out your strengths.

And, although I speak of the wife whose husband has strayed, these same strategies can apply to a man whose wife is cheating. But remember: This book should not be used by philanderers or those who want to cheat. The purpose of this book is to help people who fear adultery, not to aid adulterers.

Discover the facts, analyze the consequences, evaluate your options, and take action. Instead of precipitating a chain of unhappy events, think before you act. Without knowing the truth and what your options are, you can't take charge of your destiny.

1

IS HE CHEATING?

Fidelity has a different meaning for men than it has for women. Why is it so important to you?

To most women, there is one standard of loyalty, sexual fidelity. A man who has sex with someone else is unfaithful and disloyal, regardless of anything else he does or doesn't do. A man who loses his paycheck at the track or refuses to go to his daughter's graduation is still considered a loyal husband as long as he doesn't have sex with another woman.

You can discover your husband's adultery potential if you know his views of fidelity, excuses men use, their cheating patterns, and the various types of affairs.

HIS VIEW OF FIDELITY

The male view of loyalty is more complex because it isn't based just on sex. To him, loyalty includes emotional and financial fidelity, even though he doesn't use these terms or conceptualize loyalty in this manner.

Fidelity means to a man that his wife and family come first, but not exclusively.

Financial Fidelity

When a woman spends her husband's paycheck in a way other than the one he wants, he feels she's disloyal. If he objects to purple outfits, lottery tickets, or gifts to her bratty nephew, and she spends money on them anyway, he's going to resent her.

Emotional Fidelity

If a man reveals his dreams and frustrations, he does so with a woman. Unless he's still a mama's boy, or is in the throes of an affair, the woman with whom he is sharing his inner-most thoughts is his wife.

Men don't reveal their intimate thoughts to other men.

And contrary to what you may have thought, they don't talk about their wives' sexual performances, even when they're chatting with their locker-room buddies.

Women handle their emotional needs differently. Their confidantes are not their husbands, but their female friends. A woman shares her feelings with colleagues she knows through work, school, or the neighborhood. As a result, she's having conversations with her friends that he will not likely have with his buddies.

A simple, almost insignificant matter such as a chat with a neighbor could be construed by a husband as emotional infidelity. He might view these informal talks as opportunities to disclose family secrets, and think that you're being disloyal. If he's sensitive, your husband might view your heart-to-heart conversations with your girlfriends as a threat to your marriage.

Keeping His Secrets

As an example: your husband has been working at the plant with Jim for five years. Three years ago, Jim and his wife, Doris, moved into your neighborhood. You and she have since become close friends. Which of these five statements would you make to Doris?

1. "My husband sprained his back fixing the sink on Saturday, and I had to spend Sunday nursing him back to health."
2. "I'm so proud of my husband. Next week, he's supposed to get a big promotion."

3. "My mother's ill, so I'll be staying with her for a few weeks."
4. "My husband can't sleep when he watches horror movies late at night."
5. "My daughter is flunking algebra."

These statements seem like ordinary conversation between you and Doris, but your husband could find something wrong with any one of them, and he might feel that you're saying something disloyal.

He could be bothered by the first statement because he'll worry that his boss might hear that he has a health problem. Even worse, the story makes him look incompetent in household repairs. And while he will not talk to others about his sex life with you, he would let his buddies speculate as to the cause of his bad back.

In the second situation, you're praising him, but he might be annoyed because you're revealing secrets. Now he'll worry that Jim will sabotage his promotion and try to get it for himself.

The third situation could be embarrassing to him, too. Other men, including Jim, who will hear it from Doris, might think you are leaving him, and his buddies could make snide comments about you going home to your mother.

The fourth is too personal to discuss with a friend, according to the male perspective. After all, he doesn't discuss anything about you in bed with his buddies.

Even the fifth statement isn't suitable. He'll take this criticism of his daughter as a negative reflection of his mental abilities.

From your standpoint, you've had a nice, pleasant conversation with a close friend, but from his standpoint, you've been telling secrets and betraying him.

You're astounded that your husband is upset; that was never your intention.

On the other hand, he cannot understand that you're distressed over his sexual contact with another. Jeopardizing your marriage was the last thing on his mind.

DISCOVERING HIS ADULTERY POTENTIAL

You can discover how likely your husband is to have an affair; his attitudes and behavior will give you the crucial clues. For simplicity, we can divide men into three categories when it comes to infidelity potential: some are questing, others are merely receptive, and still others are actively attempting to be faithful. However, even men in this third category are vulnerable to spontaneous affairs.

Questors

He's out on the prowl even though he has a wife at home. Men in this category have already justified (to themselves, not their wives) their search for a casual sexual contact or even a mistress. They feel polygamy is their birthright.

Receptive Men

Some men are ready, willing, and able to have affairs, but aren't looking for these opportunities. If the right woman—or even the wrong one—takes the initiative and pursues him, he'll be receptive. How could he turn away a desirable woman who falls into his lap?

A man who is receptive to advances, but wouldn't pursue another woman, is like someone who wouldn't steal, but would keep valuables that he found. He's less likely to have an affair than a man who's looking to cheat, but you shouldn't assume that your husband is faithful just because he isn't looking for action.

Men Who Are Trying to Be Faithful

A number of men are trying hard to be faithful. It may not come naturally to them, but they're making the effort. Actually, this category is larger than the other two. When a man marries, it is usually his intention to forsake all other women.

Nevertheless, a man who is trying to be honorable might be having an affair. He may have failed in his efforts, and may feel guilty, but the affair happens.

In fact, men who are trying to be faithful are vulnerable to spontaneous affairs—liaisons that happen suddenly, without any planning, at least on their part.

EXCUSES MEN USE

Men who cheat have reasons. There are the real causes, the excuses they make to themselves, and the explanations they give others. As a wife, you might feel that none of these justifies adultery, especially by your husband. If you want to stop cheating, or better yet, prevent it, you need to know more about these reasons.

These are twenty-five reasons why men cheat, or say they're cheating:

1. *Need for Sex.* Some men cheat because they don't get enough sex at home. Some women forget that sex is a need, and that the opposite side of the fidelity coin is an obligation to keep their spouses sexually satisfied. Just as a hungry man seeks a restaurant, a horny man seeks a sexual companion.

2. *Ego.* Some husbands have sex with other women to boost their egos. For them sex represents acceptance, recognition, or praise. Other men view their sexual activity as a form of conquest, and view their activity as an accomplishment or achievement. Such men judge themselves on the basis of their popularity with women.

3. *Boredom.* Some men have affairs because they're just plain bored. If he's tired of his job and his wife, yet he's too active for chess and too sedentary for tennis, he might have an affair to fill up his idle time. His mistress may be his hobby. He'll say to himself that his friends spend time away from home when they go hunting and fishing, and he'll equate those recreational hours with the ones he spends with his mistress.

4. *Opportunity*. A man might try to realize the goals he set for himself in his youth, even if they are no longer appropriate. If he dreamed of traveling the world, he might put his career on hold to fulfill that fantasy. Similarly, when he was a fifteen-year-old, pimply-faced boy, he dreamed of beautiful women desiring him. If a woman tries to seduce him, it's a real fulfillment of a teenage dream. He might put his marriage on the back burner and seize the opportunity. He has had his years of famine, and now he is going to feast.

5. *Spontaneity*. When it comes to sexual attraction, there *is* such a thing as spontaneous combustion. Love at first sight is quite rare, but lust at first sight is commonplace. His excuse is likely to be, "I didn't plan it. It just happened."

6. *Habit*. Like overeating or drinking to excess, philandering can become a habit. He may be saying to himself, "I've always had affairs, so why should I stop now?"

7. *Cleverness*. Some men have affairs because they like the feeling of getting away with something. They want to show that they can outwit and outsmart the people around them. Men with this attitude are likely to cheat on their income taxes, shortchange their customers, and overstate their assets when they're applying for a loan.

8. *Anger at Society*. Because fidelity is supposed to be the norm, a man might have an affair as a way of thumbing his nose at society. If a man feels that he is not fully accepted by his peers because of his short stature, foreign accent, lack of education, clumsiness, or homeliness, or for some other reason, he might be seeking revenge on society. Having an affair may be his method of getting even.

9. *Anger at His Wife.* A husband who's angry at his wife might show this emotion in a number of ways, including cheating. For instance, a man who is furious with his wife because she invited her mother to move in is a likely candidate to seek revenge by having an affair.

10. *Quest for a New Spouse.* Some men hate being single. If they don't like their wives, they won't seek divorces without having another woman ready to comfort them. They will actively seek their new lovers before getting rid of their mates.

11. *Rejection of Fidelity.* Not everyone believes in fidelity. Some men reject the concept that marriage means never having sex with another woman.

12. *Recreation.* Some men choose sex as their favorite recreational activity. A husband's quest for sexual activity might be put ahead of fidelity, but he views his marriage as a serious commitment. He's not seeking a new mate, he is looking for sport.

13. *Adventure.* For some people, danger is an aphrodisiac. Instead of hunting wild animals, exploring the oceans, or climbing mountains, a lot of men gain a sense of adventure from having affairs. For them, the risk of getting caught just adds to the excitement.

14. *True Love.* According to some men, true love has to overcome many obstacles, including marriage. When a man believes that he has met his ideal mate, he might not let his present status stand in his way. Such a man views himself as an incurable romantic, rather than as a philanderer.

15. *Wife's Incapacity.* When a woman becomes ill, her husband might feel driven to an affair, whether for sex or solace. The length of the wife's illness before he will seek an affair differs from one man to another. Some men might hold off for years, but others might wait just weeks or even days.

16. *Conformity.* Some men believe that all their friends are philandering. Moreover, they feel that this situation justifies their affairs. They're conformists, not romantics.

17. *Newness.* Curiosity and then sexual desire can be sparked by the unknown. Many men enjoy the additional impetus and sexual pleasure it brings. Others find it absolutely necessary for their performance. Either way, the quest for newness leads to affairs. If there's any consolation, these men are not true to anyone.

18. *Companionship.* Some men seek friendship, and if they find this kind of relationship with a woman, it may lead to an affair even if the man had no thoughts of having one.

19. *Fear of Exclusivity.* Some men don't want to put all their emotional eggs in the same basket. They are afraid of being hurt, so they divide their ties between two or more women.

20. *Lack of Control.* Fidelity takes self-control, and some men lack the discipline necessary to be a loyal husband. They'll make some other excuse, but this is the reality. They just can't say no!

21. *Altruism*. He might claim that he's doing a good deed by having sex with her. Perhaps she's new in town and doesn't know anyone else. Or he might say that there are too many women and too few men. Husbands who use these clichés believe that the statements are true and that their behavior is justified.

22. *Old Times' Sake*. Some married men wouldn't think of starting a new affair, but reviving an old one is a different matter. If he runs into his prior mistress or just a woman who's an old flame, he might have sex with her for sentimental value. He knows he's supposed to forsake all others, and he feels that he's already met this requirement because he had already forsaken her.

23. *Same Time, Next Year*. Some men feel that an extramarital relationship is justifiable as long as the trysts are infrequent. If they meet each year at an industry's convention or their class reunion, he'll feel this relationship is appropriate. He tells himself, "After all, my wife has me the other three hundred and sixty-four days of the year."

24. *Because Their Wives Do*. If a man discovers that his wife is cheating, he probably isn't going to kill her or her lover, but he's going to feel justified in doing the same thing she is, even if he's never been unfaithful before.

25. *Lack of Interest*. A man might use his lack of interest in a woman as an excuse for having an affair with her. Initially, this idea seems strange, and it *is*. When a man isn't really drawn to a woman, he thinks of her as "safe"—someone who won't endanger his marriage. He wouldn't do anything that would risk his marriage, but he's concluded that there's no risk with her.

CHEATING PATTERNS

These vary substantially from one man to another. Before you can determine whether your husband is cheating, you'll need to know about the four basic patterns.

Prostitutes

Some men hire these women, meeting them in bars or on the streets, often in neighborhoods that are known for their hooker hangouts. A man who has sex with a prostitute justifies his actions on the basis that he's minimizing the risk of emotional involvements that could jeopardize his marriage.

He's also spending money that could otherwise be used to benefit his family. If he's wealthy, he'll claim that his family doesn't need the money. In any event, he'll compare the amount he spends on prostitutes with the amount his wife spends on herself, or he'll compare the amount he spends on her with the amount he saves by not buying an expensive "toy."

Call Girls

There's a big difference between call girls and prostitutes—call girls are far more expensive. More important, repeat contact often takes place, as the man requests the same woman. With this continuity comes bonding. Even though the call girl has a number of clients, the man eventually develops some measure of affection for her.

At some point, he will try to rationalize the amount of money being spent on the call girl. From his standpoint, he's not paying for services, he is just giving gifts to a friend.

He justifies his contact with the call girl on the basis that he's protecting his family's health, his basis of comparison being the prostitute, not his wife. As flawed as this reasoning might appear, it has some validity for a man who has been frequenting prostitutes.

Dating

Married men are part of the dating scene. Some men who appear to be single and searching are really married and looking. They're meeting women at cultural events, recreational activities, and singles bars, as well as through classified ads and video dating services. On dates, they go to dinner and the movies, and often to bed.

When they first meet, he might be less than candid, telling

her where he is from and where he is going, but leaving out certain details, such as his marital status and perhaps his real name.

A woman who becomes involved with a married man is often unaware of the man's marital status until their relationship becomes serious. The man doesn't want her to know that he's married until the bonding process is well underway. This kind of man plans to keep his wife until someone better comes along.

Mistresses

Here the term *mistress* describes a steady lover with some degree of mutual exclusivity. Money usually doesn't change hands, and typically, the mistress isn't "kept." There is at least a pretense of affection, and the mistress usually sees herself as the next wife.

WHERE AFFAIRS TAKE PLACE

Affairs are consummated in the oddest places, from airplane restrooms to abandoned subway stations, from church pews to funeral parlors, but most affairs have more mundane locales. There are ten places where affairs usually occur.

The Mistress's Home

Most affairs are consummated in the mistress's apartment or house. In some cases, the man will even have a key. However, some women are concerned about the neighbors' prying eyes, and won't bring him there. Also, her neighbors might recognize him, so greater discretion and secrecy become necessary. Married women with children rarely use their own places, and married women without children are still reluctant to take chances at home.

The Husband's Home

Few men are so foolhardy (or from their point of view, courageous) that they bring their mistresses home. But it does happen. When the wife is away, the mistress makes herself at home. The husband might be using the guest room with his mistress, but he might also be using the room he shares with his wife. The marital home is often the place of last resort, since the husband knows that the wife's anger will be multiplied many times if she discovers the mistress has been in the family abode.

A Parked Car

Though these are popular with teenagers, adults usually expect greater comfort for their trysts than vehicles can provide. As cars have become smaller, their lovemaking potential has decreased. But look for footprints on his car ceiling. If he cleans the car interior frequently, he could be preparing to meet her or destroying evidence.

A Pied-à-terre

There are men who have their own secret hideaways, but they are few and far between. Most men have enough trouble paying their share of monthly expenses at home and don't have funds left over for an extra apartment or cabin. Borrowing an apartment from a friend is an option.

A Company Apartment

Some companies maintain guest apartments, but they aren't all that common. Besides, most are supposed to be used for business guests, not mistresses. Use of the company apartment is a perk for higher-ups, and isn't available for just anyone.

Hotels and Motels

Motels that are suitable for business travelers and vacation-ers are the most popular with husbands and mistresses. They will rarely frequent quickie motels, since they are used by hookers and their johns, not by lovers. No-tell motels look cheap, but if they are the only accommodations avail-able, they will be used. Yes, once in a while he will splurge on an expensive room in a fine hotel—but not often.

At the Office

Empty offices are rarely used for trysts, but the possibility continues to tantalize illicit lovers. If your husband seems unusually knowledgeable about office cleaning schedules, alarm systems, or watchmen schedules, find out why.

In an RV

Recreational vehicles have become increasingly popular for liaisons. Vans and motor homes have been used for sexual encounters, as have boats.

At a Friend's Home

A mistress might not have a place of her own, possibly because she is living with her parents, children, or husband. In that event, the husband and his mistress may be using a friend's apartment. Of course, if they're seeing each other frequently, using a friend's apartment is too cumbersome. Beside, friends who are that discreet are hard to find.

The Great Outdoors

Nature provides some lovely and private areas for lovers. If you notice a little more mileage on the car or some unexplained pine needles, you should wonder where he was.

TYPES OF AFFAIRS

If your husband is having an affair, don't expect it to end on its own. You can't just wish it away.

Some will end without your interference, others will stop only if you terminate them, while still others won't finish no matter what you do. If you still want your husband, you'll need to know what type of affair he's having.

Once a relationship reaches the level of an affair, it has some measure of regularity or permanence.

Permanent Affairs

Some affairs last for decades—longer than many marriages—so it's accurate to call them permanent. This type can survive anguish or illness, or almost anything short of death or divorce. Typically, the man and the woman in this situation have decided that they will never marry each other, so there's no pressure on the husband to leave his wife. Often they live in different cities or have vastly different backgrounds. If he does divorce his wife, or if she dies, that event then threatens the stability of the affair. Either they will marry or split up, but they won't continue as is.

Transitional Affairs

Many affairs are transitional. The husband tells the other woman that he'll leave his wife after some specified event, such as the birth of his child. He tells her, "I can't leave my wife while she's pregnant." In some cases, the husband does leave his wife after this occurrence, but more often than not, a new event takes its place. Twenty years later, he may be telling her that he'll leave his wife as soon as his child finishes college. It may take her a while to discover that he's misleading her.

Temporary Affairs

Some affairs are meant to be short-lived. The husband doesn't say to the other woman that he'll be leaving his wife; he tells her that the relationship will end when his wife returns from her skiing trip or her overseas visit. Or, the other woman may have her own agenda and schedule. There's no overt threat to the marriage, since she's not pushing for a change in the relationship.

TEST YOURSELF I

Assume that there is no evidence your husband is cheating. How would you handle these situations? Take this quiz. Your answers will help you evaluate your reactions.

Mark the answers that best describe your feelings on a separate sheet of paper.

QUIZ

1. At the supermarket, you are surprised to see your husband because he didn't tell you that he would be there. How would you respond?
   a. Tell him what you need.
   b. Accuse him of looking for other women.
   c. Apologize for not buying what he likes.
   d. Look in his shopping cart to determine if there are products you don't use.

2. At the same supermarket, you observe your husband talking to a woman you don't recognize. How would you react to her?

a. Run into her shopping cart.

b. Introduce yourself as his wife.

c. Leave the store.

d. Buy gourmet food.

3. At the supermarket, your husband is chatting with one of your neighbors—a woman who is younger than you are. How do you react?

a. Tell her that you are terrific.

b. Join the conversation.

c. Wave from a distance.

d. Indicate to your husband to stop talking.

4. Your husband is a contractor. You observe him at a restaurant with a woman. What should you do?

a. Ask them about their potential contract.

b. Ignore the situation.

c. Go to a fancier restaurant.

d. Walk in and accuse him of flirting.

5. Your husband wants to go out with the boys each Wednesday. What is your reaction?

a. Go out with your women friends to a better place.

b. Boys will be boys.

c. Go out with your men friends.

d. Ask him about his friends.

6. There's a message for your husband on your answering machine from a woman. You don't recognize her name. What would you do?

   a. Call her yourself to determine what she wants.
   b. Erase the message.
   c. Ignore the message.
   d. Give your husband a cross-examination about her.

7. One of your husband's co-workers, an attractive single woman, is in the hospital. Your husband wants to visit her. How would you react?
   a. Remind him he never visited his sister when she was sick.
   b. Go with him.
   c. Tell him he never took care of you when you were ill.
   d. Give him a book to take to her.

8. Your husband returns from a three-day business conference in a different city. He says he lost his wedding ring when he left it on the bathroom counter. How do you react?
   a. Buy him a new ring.
   b. Cry.
   c. Buy an expensive ring for yourself.
   d. Accuse him of "playing single."

9. Your husband suddenly develops an interest in gourmet cooking. You react by:
   a. Accusing him of just wanting to meet other women.
   b. Recognizing his greater ability to learn than yours.
   c. Telling him he should try to surpass your skills in some area.
   d. Agreeing that you should both learn gourmet cooking.

10. You discover that your husband has been hiding large sums of money? What do you do?

    a. Ignore what he has been doing.
    b. Think he is cheating, so you should do the same.
    c. Ask him for the money.
    d. Find out why he is hiding money.

11. Your husband wants you to change your appearance:
    a. Tell him "I choose what I wear."
    b. Assume he wants you to look like his mistress.
    c. Ask him to go shopping with you.
    d. Accede to his demands.

12. Your husband starts calling you "Mom." What do you do?
    a. Tell him you are not his mother.
    b. Assume you've lost sex appeal.
    c. Call him "Mom."
    d. Tell him you look young enough to be his daughter.

13. He suddenly becomes concerned about his appearance. What do you do?
    a. Update your own wardrobe and image before he can improve his.
    b. Tell him he is fat and bald.
    c. Tell him he's right for you.
    d. Believe he's trying to impress a woman.

14. Your husband is suddenly bored at work. What do you do?
    a. Tell him to take a newspaper.
    b. Tell him your job is tougher and you don't complain.
    c. Meet him for lunch every few days until his mood changes.
    d. Accuse him of philandering and preferring play to work.

15. Your husband is helping your new neighbors move in. He spent an hour and a half helping the wife do something that should have taken forty-five minutes. Your reaction is:

a. Ask what took so much time.

b. Accuse him of being infatuated with her.

c. Serve him a cold soda.

d. Flirt with your neighbor's husband.

ANSWERS

	A Wimpy	B Egocentric	C Angry	D Practical
1.	c	a	b	d
2.	c	d	a	b
3.	c	a	d	b
4.	b	c	d	a
5.	b	a	c	d
6.	c	b	d	a
7.	d	c	a	b
8.	b	c	d	a
9.	b	c	a	d
10.	a	c	b	d
11.	d	a	b	c
12.	b	d	c	a
13.	d	a	b	c
14.	a	b	d	c
15.	c	d	b	a

Add up your answers and you'll see what category your responses place you in. Although your answers won't all fall into one category, the majority of one type of response will reflect one of four personality types—wimpy, practical, angry, and egocentric.

When a woman believes that her husband may be cheating, she often causes an unnecessary rift in the marriage. Three of these categories predict marital strife.

Wimpy

If most of your answers were in column A, you are so lacking in self-esteem or so afraid of confrontation that it won't be long before your marriage is in trouble, since you're too ready to believe your husband is cheating. You rarely express yourself because you're trying to avoid arguments. Your assumptions about him could be unpleasant, so you will just walk out of the relationship. If your marriage is fading, you won't tell your mate. He is shocked to discover your unhappiness when you pull away.

He may view your passivity as a sign that you have no interest in him. As a result, he may start planning his way out of the marriage. You must discuss your fears with him, or suspicions will destroy you.

Egocentric

If your answers were mostly in column B, your selfishness makes you think you can dazzle him with your power, splendor, and importance.

Competing with your husband is good as long as it's between yourselves and in private. However, you must stand with him against the world. If he realizes that you always want the limelight and will push him aside for your benefit, it won't be long before you're his enemy. You are creating the desire for adultery rather than stopping it.

Angry

If your responses are mostly in column C, and you haven't even proven his adultery, you're asking for a self-fulfilling prophecy. Your wrath will lead him to another woman.

Angry responses are acceptable occasionally. At least your husband knows you're not indifferent to him. If anything, you care too much.

Practical

If your responses fall into column D, you are in the best position to gather information necessary to reach your goals. You generally give your mate a chance to explain what he did and why he did it, and he doesn't fear emotional outburst from you. Your communications are wide open. More often than not, there's an acceptable reason why your husband behaved the way he did, and you have no cause to be angry. If you understand his behavior, you are better equipped to predict what he will do in the future. You are in the best position to monitor any potential adultery and remedy the situation.

2

PROVING HIS INFIDELITY

If you're serious about discovering whether your husband is cheating—and with whom—you should observe him closely. His behavior doesn't always indicate what you think it does. Use the tools that are readily available to you—everything from your senses to government records—to investigate him yourself.

THEY AREN'T ALWAYS AS THEY SEEM

Your husband's behavior may mean something very different from what it implies. Surprisingly, what seems innocent can be devastating, and what seems harmful can be helpful. Let's look at some of these situations.

Sex Magazines

One day, when you're in the basement looking for an article about affordable vacations, you notice a stack of magazines on your husband's desk. These publications have pictures of white, sandy beaches, but the women enjoying them are in various states of undress. In fact, the real focus of the magazine is the sexy parts of the female body.

People sometimes utilize these magazines to fulfill desires that aren't being satisfied in real life. If you try to stop this outlet, he'll be more likely to seek out other women with whom he can fulfill his fantasies.

By now, you're probably thinking that your husband is a philanderer, or worse. But the reality is otherwise. In fact, your husband's interest in sex magazines might even indicate that he's *not* cheating.

He's gazing at these magazines because he wants more and better sex. If you want him to lose interest in these magazines, offer your own sexuality. Tell him you saw a photo in a magazine that turned you on. Suggest that he show you some of his favorite pictures. It can increase the sexuality you can share together.

When He's Traveling

Check up on him. When he says he is staying at a certain hotel, make sure that he is where he says he is. Don't let him call you; phone him instead. If in doubt, check the number to see if he's really at a hotel. When you speak with him, coax him to confess to you how much he loves you, misses you, wants to make love to you. Make him tell you that you're the only person he wants to be with. He won't be able to say these things if the other woman is there. His excuse may be that he can't talk because his male colleagues are with him in the room. If this is his reply, request to speak to one of them, just to get his reaction. Then call him back later, tell him that you're amorous, and ask him to talk of love. He'll be stymied if she's still there.

Your Gifts

Beware if your husband starts giving you more presents. It may mean that he's having an affair and trying to compensate for his actions. If he feels guilty, he's likely to bring you flowers, candy, jewelry, or other frivolous or pricey items. Since he's giving you less of himself, he wants to give you more "things" to make up for your loss.

34

Gifts to Her

If your husband is seeing another woman on a regular basis, he might be buying her presents. You might not recognize the significance of this unless you know more about relationships and gifts. Here are the basics.

A man who's consorting and cavorting with prostitutes is paying directly for services. Cash changes hands, but gifts are rare. If he's hiring a call girl, he might be giving her presents instead of cash to establish a pretense that he isn't buying her services. She will demand articles that are readily convertible into cash, such as gold, bearer bonds, or tickets to a rock concert.

If he's dating a number of women, he's likely to be giving them candy and flowers, especially on those occasions when he would like to be with them but can't be, perhaps because he is with you. If he has a mistress of long standing, he probably gives her practical gifts, not just candy and flowers, like a set of steak knives, a television, or an accessory for her car. The more costly and/or practical the gift, the longer he has been seeing her.

Condoms

Many marriages have come to an abrupt halt when the wife has found a condom in the husband's personal possessions.

The condoms were often found in wallets, but sometimes in money belts, socks, briefcases, or glove compartments. Don't assume that your husband is cheating just because you find a condom.

A man might keep one "for emergencies." It might have been in his wallet since his high school days. A symbol of his manhood, at most, it's a statement of his sexual freedom. By having one he asserts the right to have sex with another woman, but may have the good judgment not to exercise that power.

Keep Track of His Clothing

A man who is having an affair eventually finds it more convenient to change clothes at his mistress's home. He is likely to have an extra set of underwear and socks at her house.

Most married men rely on their wives to buy their clothing. Since you are his wife, you can easily detect if his clothing disappears. You know his wardrobe far better than he does. If you ask your husband about some article of clothing you can't find, he might say that he threw it out because it was torn. But most men don't throw out their old clothes; they wait for their wives to do it for them.

If an entire set of clothes disappears at one time, it is likely that he has moved them to another woman's closet.

Lunch with a Woman

Don't assume that your husband is cheating on you just because he had lunch alone with a woman. In fact, it might even show that he isn't cheating.

Men and women are co-workers, business associates, and just friends. Lunch together might be completely innocent. Before you jump to conclusions, you need more facts: How often do they have lunch together? What type of restaurant do they frequent? When are they together aside from lunch? Are they eating near his office or hers? Is the restaurant well lit and the seating suitable for business conversations, or is the setting intimate? Do they have lunch together once every few weeks or a few times per week? Are they working on a project that would require their frequent contact?

You need to answer these questions before you know whether their togetherness is a sign of cheating. If there is no good reason for them to lunch together so often, only then assume the worst.

The Rendezvous

If you're serious about discovering your husband with another woman, you need to know what affairs are really like. The wife usually pictures a secret meeting in a dimly lit bistro with strolling violinists. She thinks of a secret password at the door and intrigue within—a rendezvous that is sordid yet glamorous, in a seamy and steamy way. If this is your view, you'll never catch your husband with another woman.

He is more likely to be meeting her in a family restaurant or even in a fast food joint. Their time is limited, so the meal will be intense. They rarely have time for glamour, and they don't want to be highly visible.

Eating Patterns

Your husband's eating habits will change once an affair begins. If he dines with her, he may not eat with you. Is your husband gaining weight? If he eats with you *and* with her, he will. His relationship with her may also affect his food preferences. When he turns down his favorite food— lasagna, for instance—he may have just had the dish with her.

Animals

Pets can tell you about your husband. Under the pretext of exercising the dog, your husband could be seeing the other woman. If your dog does not bark at another woman when she visits your home, or if it runs over to her when you're walking it in the neighborhood, the dog may already be familiar with her smell. Ask her what she did last Friday (when your husband was out) and see if she becomes nervous.

KEEPING TRACK

If you're like most women, you don't like to spy on your husband. If he kept track of your activities, you would think it was an invasion of privacy. You're observing his daily routine anyway, so all you're doing is recording your observations. You're not taking unfair advantage by keeping records—"All's fair in love and war." You're trying to uncover his manipulations to preserve your marriage.

Keeping a Diary

If you have kept one before, you can do it again. If he discovers it, and it isn't locked, don't despair. These are five explanations you can use. Tell him:

1. That he is so special he deserves all this attention.
2. You're writing his biography.
3. You're making notes of his needs and wants.
4. He acts as if he's afraid that you'll discover he's cheating.
5. You are interested in his health—his cholesterol count, allergies, or illnesses.

Your diary will be most useful if it includes chronological records and personal asides. Devote at least one page each day to these observations. Cheating follows a pattern, and you'll recognize it faster if you record activities. The few minutes it takes to record your data is well worth the fidelity protection you will receive in return.

Daily Observations

At a minimum, you should be recording the answers to these ten questions about your husband's activities every day:

1. What time did he wake up?
2. Did he bathe in the morning?
3. What did he eat in the morning?
4. When did he leave the house?
5. Did he take the car?
6. When did he return?
7. Did he eat after returning?
8. Did he bathe after returning?
9. Did he want sex with you?
10. What time did he go to bed?

Personal Observations

Here are other observations you should include in your diary:

1. *His Personality Changes.* The more time he spends with another woman, the more likely she will influence him. Look

for new interests, changes in sense of humor, a different threshold for anger, a need for privacy, and any rearrangement of priorities. Put another woman's hair on his jacket and ask him how it got there. Watch his response.

2. *His Energy Level.* Sex with two women takes stamina. Is he helping with the household chores, such as mowing the lawn or fixing simple plumbing problems? Is he more sedentary?

3. *His Conversational Pattern.* He won't talk freely about himself. He'll talk more about others and what he reads or sees on television.

4. *His Sexual Needs.* Is he still an ardent lover, both in frequency and intensity?

5. *His Appetite.* With added sex, he'll eat foods that have a fast energy effect, such as sweets, and start taking high-potency vitamins. His appetite may increase because he's using more energy.

6. *His Consideration Toward You.* Is he strongly suggesting activities for you that keep you busy or away from home? He may be looking for free time to see her or ways to keep your mind occupied.

7. *His Family Plans.* If he wants to be part of the family and spend time with the children he must plan ahead. Look for more structured rather than spontaneous family activities.

8. *His Attitudes Toward Others.* Is he shunning company and social events? He may be too busy.

9. *His Spending Patterns.* Is he carrying more cash and using credit cards less? Is he spending less on his usual interests, but not saving?

10. *His Sleeping Patterns.* If he's having sex with her, his tiredness pattern will change. He'll probably need more sleep.

Each of these observations gives you clues to his behavior when you know what to look for. Compare his actions over several months. No one alters routines dramatically overnight—and changes don't necessarily mean he's cheating.

COME TO YOUR SENSES

Your senses are very important clues to his behavior. Even the sense of smell—generally, the least important sense—can be helpful.

Using Your Sense of Smell

This sense varies greatly from one person to another. If you're fortunate enough to have a good sense of smell, you'll find it much easier to detect philandering. Here are ten examples where a telltale scent can expose a cheater:

1. He will wash up after sex with his mistress, but you detect the aroma of the soap he used, which is different from your own.
2. He leaves an extra set of underwear at his mistress's apartment, which in due time she launders. Later, when he wears clean briefs home, you can detect the aroma of a different detergent.
3. You may be able to detect the odor of a deodorant on your husband, even if his mistress was the one who used it.
4. He brushes his teeth after he has sex with his mistress, but you notice the aroma of an unusual toothpaste.
5. You discover a mistress's perfume on your husband's clothes.
6. You smell pet odors on your husband's pants and socks—and you don't have pets.
7. If your husband is nervous, he's going to sweat more, and it will be more acidic and noticeable. Watch for this clue when you talk about some topic that makes him uncomfortable, such as infidelity.
8. Cosmetics have aromas, too. Even if traces of her makeup, aren't visible you may be able to detect the scent on your husband's clothes.
9. You might discover the hint of her hairspray on your husband's clothes.
10. And, another woman's body odor will linger on skin and clothing.

If your husband didn't have the opportunity to wash, change his clothes, or remove telltale smells, he will probably head directly for the bathroom to freshen up as soon as he arrives home. That is a clue in itself.

Don't worry if you can't identify specific brand names.

You're only looking for scents that didn't come from your home.

GOVERNMENTAL RECORDS

A philandering husband is hard to track. If he isn't where he is supposed to be, how do you know where he is—and with whom? One of your sources is governmental records. There are various types, such as:

1. *Driver's License.* Look at his license. It will tell you data about him that you might need later such as points for violations. If you are in doubt, contact the Department of Motor Vehicles for his records.

2. *Parking Tickets.* These can often give you clues to his whereabouts, because they will reflect time and place. But be careful in using your husband's parking tickets because he might not have been the driver—he might have loaned his car to a friend or business associate. Once you know your husband's whereabouts, you can piece it together with other information to prove his adultery.

3. *Moving Violations.* Look for tickets. Speeding or other moving violation tickets should indicate the time, date, and location of the offense. He can't deny his whereabouts and when he was stopped.

4. *Arrest Records.* If your husband has ever been arrested, ask for a copy of his record. You can obtain this from the police by filling out a request and paying a nominal fee. The record should show the date, time, and place of the arrest, and indicate who was with him. It will also show the circumstances surrounding his arrest, and perhaps his blood alcohol level.

5. *Passport and Visa.* If your husband travels from one country to another, governments are likely to stamp his passport when he arrives and leaves. In addition, some countries require extensive documentation for entry, including how much money a person is carrying. These records provide useful information as to his whereabouts and real reason for travel. If he tells you he's on a business trip and you see "tourist" visas stamped on his passport, ask him to explain them.

6. *Court Files.* Has he ever been involved in a lawsuit? If he's a divorced man, he probably has been. The papers from his divorce can be very enlightening because the reason for the breakup may have been adultery.

7. *Real Estate Records.* Kept at the local courthouse, these papers reveal when your husband owned property and with whom, and might indicate the amounts he paid or received. These records can also verify what he has told you about himself. You may discover he owned a house with a woman, who had to be more than a casual friend or fling.

8. *Tax Returns.* These indicate income, but you're more interested in what he did with the money.

9. *Birth Certificate.* This document obviously gives you the date and place of his birth. You would be surprised to know how many men don't admit their true ages. If you are not sure about how old he is, look at his birth certificate. His true age may explain his behavior.

10. *Voter Registration.* If your husband registers to vote, he will have to provide verified information about himself. Looking at his card, you can double-check his date of birth, his party affiliation, and the date he first registered to vote in that area. New registrations are issued periodically and the old cards are tossed in a drawer. Those old cards can provide a history of his past legal residences. You may discover an address you don't recognize.

CONTACTING THE TAX AUTHORITIES

If your husband is cheating on you, he could also be cheating on his taxes. You are so angry at him, you might be tempted to report him to the tax authorities. Should you turn him in? In most cases you are better off if you don't.

His Mistress's Expenses

Your husband's tax cheating is related to his marital infidelity. When he takes his mistress to dinner and then to the theater, he might treat the event as a business outing, and claim a deduction for all or part of these costs. In addition, he might write off the cost of traveling to see her, whether he uses public transportation or his car.

Look at his records. If you know about his business,

clients, and colleagues, you'll know whether he is seeing her for strictly business matters.

If your husband is providing all or part of his mistress's living expenses, he might be claiming improper tax deductions. For example, he might claim that presents to her are business gifts. If he's paying her rent, it might show up on his accounting records as office space or a guest apartment. If he's giving her money, he might even treat these amounts as salaries or wages "for services rendered." "Consulting," "typing services," and "escort services" might not be what they appear to be.

Start your inquiries with his accounting records. He should have receipts to prove his expenses. If he makes excuses, keeping the receipts from you, something is up.

His Taxes and You

Your tax situation is quite different from your personal circumstances since your husband might have income that he doesn't report to the tax authorities. He might be hiding his money from you to pay for his personal activities. If he's an executive, professional, or technician, he'll have opportunities as a consultant or for part-time work. He might be spending some of his spare time earning extra money as well as philandering with his mistress.

If you could demonstrate that your husband is cheating on his taxes, the authorities are likely to go after him. But what happens when they do? They're not going to help you in proving adultery and they're not likely to give you a reward.

Don't start what you can't stop. After you've contacted the

tax authorities, you might reconcile with your husband. You can't tell the tax authorities to forget about your information, or that you were only kidding.

To make matters worse, the tax authorities are likely to enlist your cooperation for hearings again, which would further exacerbate your relationship with your husband. They will make your husband pay fines and interest, as well as back taxes. Less will be left for you and the children.

You might have to pay, too. You could claim that you are the innocent spouse and you know nothing about his activities, but you have the burden of proof and it's difficult to prove. You sign the tax returns; you are responsible.

Her Taxes

Although it's rarely worthwhile to report your husband to the tax authorities, reporting his mistress is a different matter. If his "gifts" to her are really payments for services rendered, she is supposed to report them as income. Items such as watches and televisions that are given for services aren't treated as gifts—they count as income. She also should be paying taxes if your husband gives her a rent-free apartment.

You're unlikely to get the evidence to present to the tax authorities. However, if you do, its impact on her is likely to be serious. She knows you're not going to be a pushover.

Cheating the Company

Your husband might be cheating the company he works for, as well. You should think twice about telling the company that he put his woman on the payroll, or is seeing her at the company apartment. If you squeal, he might be fired, and you might lose financially.

INVESTIGATING HIM

This could prove to be worthwhile. Consider, for instance, how to use florists. You could then modify the technique to probe his secret life.

Flowers

If your husband is seeing another woman, he's likely to be giving her flowers. Investigating florists could prove to be worthwhile. Here's an example of how to conduct an investigation of florists. (You can then modify the technique to probe other facets of his life.)

First, compile a list of florists he might be using. The florist might be near *your* home, *his* office, *her* office, *her* home, or somewhere between. Also, he might be using a different florist when he's *sending* flowers than when he's *bringing* them personally. If these possibilities seem endless, don't fret. You can narrow them down quickly.

Your husband might use a florist near your home because his presence there is not suspicious if a neighbor sees him. If he's seen, he'll simply buy flowers for you. If you've ever received an unexpected bouquet, this might be the reason. Most men won't use a florist near their homes. They're afraid they'll be spotted buying flowers everyone knows you don't like, your local florist will gossip, or a neighbor will ask you, "Where are the flowers your husband bought?"

Talk to your local florist, just to be sure. Show him a picture of you and your husband. Otherwise, describe him. Then tell the florist that your husband often brings you flowers, and that if he has a chance to make suggestions to your husband, you would like him to keep your preferences in mind. A few weeks later, go back and say a friendly hello. If he sold your husband flowers, he may remember when and talk about it.

If you suspect a specific woman, check florists near her workplace. This trail is likely to be cold unless she's married. If she's single, she wants her flowers at home.

If he's bringing her flowers, he will pick them up near her home. That way, he will only be seen in public with them for a short time. But to catch him, you must know the neighborhood where she lives.

Since there are occasions when he will send flowers because he can't be with her (such as holidays), check the florists near his office. Start there if you're looking for proof. Your best approach is to say your husband gave you flowers that were so beautiful, you want to send the exact same arrangement to his mother. See if the florist can track down the order.

Obtaining proof from a florist isn't going to be easy. He or she may try to maintain customer confidentiality (after all, your husband isn't the only one who might be cheating). To make matters more difficult, he or she might not even know your husband because the orders come in by phone.

His Keys

If your husband is having a long-term affair, and his mistress is seeing him exclusively, he is likely to have a key to her apartment. Examine your husband's key chain and take inventory of his keys. Identify where each one goes. He won't miss his key chain while he's watching a football game. Make copies of the keys you can't identify and ask him what they open. The one he says belongs to his locker at the health club might be to his mistress's apartment.

You could possibly be able to put this information to good use. If you decide to hire an investigator, he can take much better pictures of the couple leaving or entering her home when he knows exactly which doorway is hers.

Investigators

You can hire an investigator, but it might not be worth it. You can't ask your friends' advice because one of them may be the other woman or won't keep your secret. And investigation becomes costly because you're paying for time. However, even if you don't get any information about cheating, you're paying for peace of mind. Remember: if you employ an investigator, don't rule out women. In some cases, they will have more access to men.

Reverse Directory

Examine your husband's telephone bills and his telephone credit card statements. You'll discover various numbers you don't recognize. One of these numbers is likely to belong to his mistress, but which one? Check out the repeating calls.

In many cities, you'll be able to obtain a reverse telephone directory, which lists telephone numbers in numerical order and provides the name and address of the person in whose name the phone is listed. Your library may have reverse directories; if not, your librarian can tell you where you can find them. Use this reference to check out phone numbers you don't recognize.

Paper Trail

Look for slips of paper in his jacket, shirt, pants, and wallet. Check his private phone books at home and in the office (when you can) for names that seem inappropriate. His appointment book, telephone memos, and desk calendars are informative. Don't overlook the most obvious, namely matchbooks and parking receipts—men tend to return to the same restaurants.

Pursuing Him

If you discover he cheated, then let's evaluate how damaging his actions may be to your relationship and what you really want to do about it. Fidelity takes continuous effort, on your part and on his.

TEST YOURSELF II

This quiz is based on what your behavior would be if, in fact, you knew that your husband was having an affair. On a separate sheet of paper, mark down the answers that most closely describe what you would do, say, or feel if faced with the circumstances given.

QUIZ

1. Your husband wants to tell you about his affair. Should you listen to what he says about her?
   a. Yes—he has freedom of speech.
   b. Yes—get the information and use it against him.
   c. No—you don't want to know this.
   d. No—he's lying anyway.

2. If you hear what he has to say, what should you do?
   a. Denounce her in vitriolic terms.
   b. Show no interest.
   c. Tell him that he can't keep up this double life.
   d. Tell him how terrific you are.

3. If he tells you that she is terrific and beautiful, what should you do?
   a. Counteract what he has to say.
   b. Tell him you only know her bad side.
   c. Tell him if she is so terrific she will look elsewhere.
   d. Tell him you are terrific and even better.

4. If you meet her at your women's club, your reaction would be to:
   a. Be polite but leave.
   b. Find out what you can about her intentions.
   c. Tell her you are terrific.
   d. Scream "slut" at her.

5. You see your husband and the other woman together. What do you do?
   a. You don't let them see you—you hide.
   b. Give your husband a passionate kiss.
   c. Tell him he is a "cheater" in public.
   d. Tell him later that "She looks like my mother."

6. You see the other woman with a man, not your husband. You:
   a. Tell your husband.
   b. Mind your own business.
   c. Flirt with the other man.
   d. Tell him that she is a slut.

7. Flowers sent by your husband to her are delivered mistakenly to you. What should you do?
  a. Thank your husband.
  b. Return them.
  c. Send them to her—from you—collect.
  d. Rip up the flowers and put them at his side of the bed.

8. You have the same hairdresser as she does. You should:
  a. Change salons.
  b. Tell your husband she was talking about the *men* in her life.
  c. Tell your hairdresser some sleaze is chasing your husband.
  d. Get a more expensive perm.

9. You find her love note in his jacket. You should:
  a. Pretend you didn't see it.
  b. Keep it to use for evidence and make copies for the family.
  c. Replace it with one of your own love notes and keep hers for evidence.
  d. Correct the grammar and mail it back to her.

10. You discover he gave her a gift. You:
  a. Ask her to return it.
  b. Demand something better for yourself.
  c. Ask your husband if she liked it.
  d. Tell your best friend about the incident.

11. His mother tells you he is cheating. You should:
  a. Tell her to mind her own business.
  b. Tell your husband what his mother said.

    c. Invite her to visit you.
    d. Tell her you already know.

12. You discover he's having an affair with one of his employees. What do you do?
    a. Fire the employee.
    b. Decide to work with your husband for a while.
    c. Call him more often.
    d. Hire a handsome young man you can make eyes at.

13. If your marriage is in trouble, you would:
    a. Buy yourself something you've always wanted so you'll feel better.
    b. Buy him something he's always wanted so he'll feel better.
    c. Go off for a weekend together.
    d. Tell him he's a loser.

14. Your husband is having an affair, and your in-laws are visiting you for a few weeks. Your response is:
    a. You're extra nice to them so they won't notice the increased tensions.
    b. You tell your husband that they are his folks so he must take care of them. You go play.
    c. Tell them about his adultery, but explain that you'll always think of them as Mom and Dad no matter what happens.
    d. Tell them what a rat their son is.

15. You win the lottery. What do you do with the money?
    a. Hide it.
    b. Tell your husband the money is yours exclusively.
    c. Share it with him.
    d. Put it in trust for him as long as he stays with you.

16. You and your husband go to his company's annual social occasion to meet and mingle with the executives and their families. This is your chance to:
  a. Shop freely instead of mingle.
  b. Publicly ridicule your husband for the affair.
  c. Tell everyone what a terrific wife you are and how much you've contributed to his success.
  d. Tell everyone how terrific he is.

17. You pick up your phone and he's talking to her. What do you do?
  a. Call her a home wrecker and demand she hang up.
  b. Quietly hang up your receiver.
  c. Take over the conversation.
  d. Listen and learn what you can.

18. Your husband calls you by the other woman's name. You should:
  a. Laugh it off.
  b. Tell him he's prematurely senile.
  c. Ask him why he called you such an ugly name.
  d. Call him by your old flame's name.

19. You find some women's panties tucked under the seat of your car. You should:
  a. Place a pair of your husband's soiled underwear and an empty pack of condoms under the seat.
  b. Cut the panties into shreds.
  c. Put your fanciest panties under the seat.
  d. Throw them away.

20. You're going to receive an award at your company's annual awards dinner. You want:

a. Your husband along, to show him you can be successful on your own.
b. Your husband there so he can take a bow when you thank him for his encouragement and wisdom.
c. Your husband absent so he'll love you for you and not your accomplishments.
d. Your husband present to remind him he never received any award of significance in his life.

ANSWERS

	A Wimpy	B Egocentric	C Angry	D Practical
1.	a	d	c	b
2.	b	d	a	c
3.	b	d	c	a
4.	a	c	d	b
5.	a	d	c	b
6.	b	c	d	a
7.	b	c	d	a
8.	a	d	c	b
9.	a	d	b	c
10.	d	b	c	a
11.	d	a	b	c
12.	c	d	a	b
13.	b	a	d	c
14.	a	b	d	c
15.	c	b	a	d
16.	a	c	b	d

	A Wimpy	**B** Egocentric	**C** Angry	**D** Practical
17.	b	c	a	d
18.	a	d	b	c
19.	d	c	b	a
20.	c	a	d	b

Your answers will follow a pattern—they will fall into one group more than into the others. If you're wimpy, you're quick to find fault with yourself, him, and the other woman. If your answers are generally in the egocentric column, it's because you feel you must outclass him to impress him. The angry and practical answers are more likely to be mixed because anger can be a natural response for even the most practical of women, and even the anguished woman can become practical to save her marriage. However, you'll still find your answers falling mostly into one category.

Wimpy

If your answers fall into category A, you are passive and probably feel helpless to change your circumstances. You will lose simply by default. Your own mate views your fatalism as massive indifference to him. Anger is at least understandable to a mate in terms of adultery. Not caring is unforgivable.

Egocentric

If your answers fall into category B, you are so concerned about yourself that you're not focused on him or the real problems of the marriage. It's unlikely that you think of yourself as a team, so why should he?

Angry

If your answers fall into category C, you may be so angry that all that matters to you is to show it. You can't control a situation if you can't master your own emotions. Don't get rid of the anger; it's justified. Be effectively angry by giving yourself some time to think and scheme.

Practical

If your answers are mostly in category D, you can use your head even when confronted with emotional situations. You stand the best chance for success by doing what brings the results that you want. You can win him back or keep him, but it is your choice.

3

THAT BASTARD

You always thought, "Not *my* husband," but somehow an affair *did* happen. He behaved like a bastard and cheated on you. You figured that if you understood him, you could forgive him.

There is another way to look at this: If you really understand him, you may not want him. But if you do, you can win him back if you change your mind and decide to keep him after all.

Your husband's personal situations can cause his philandering. Plan your responses by using his emotions, fears, and guilts.

WHY HE PHILANDERS

Your husband has caused you grief. Somewhere he was diverted from his love for you. He wandered and lost his focus. As time goes on, his sexual desirability increases because there are fewer men than women in his age group. Yet he is past his prime, and no one knows it better than you do. To understand why he is cheating, you must try to see the situation from his particular point of view.

Midlife Crisis

When your husband goes through his midlife crisis, he thinks of himself as he was, then he tries to recapture his youth. In his mind, his friends have become stodgy. He seeks new companions, a more modern look, and perhaps a younger woman to feel rejuvenated.

In his youth, your husband thought that he was going to accomplish greatness. Now, he sees that most of his dreams won't come true. If this realization is too sudden, the impact can be devastating. His disappointment could change his perspective on family and adultery simultaneously.

His midlife crisis, like puberty, has no known cure. But he will get through it, just as surely as he got through puberty. Be patient.

Age and Beauty

How important is beauty to your husband? If physical attraction is of primary importance to him, you might lose him unless you can counteract his focus. Think back to when you met. Did he want you only because of your looks? You probably also offered great companionship, and still do.

If he reminds you that you are fatter and grayer, point out his balding dome and potbelly. This is no time for you to grin and bear it in silence. Let him know that he is not immune to time. Tell him that even though he has been mistaken for his father, you still think that he is as youthful as he was the day you met. Also, repeat any compliments others pay you; let him know others find you attractive. The compliments will stick in his mind.

Younger Version

Your husband might want a woman who is like you, only younger, as your replacement. He has always enjoyed your looks and personality; now he is seeking the same attributes in a younger body. He expects that with her he can relive the good times that he shared with you—especially his vitality and sexual potency.

Such a man fears aging. He doesn't want to admit his own mortality. Here are some strategies you can use to fight back against your husband and his younger woman:

1. Give him the opportunity to relive the cherished times. Discuss the good old days and revisit the places that were fun.
2. Maintain your physical appearance. If you're at the age when you're losing color (graying hair and paler skin are showing up), this is time for hair coloring and cosmetics.
3. Dress in a more youthful manner. Go shopping with your grown children, if you have them, and let them select your outfits.
4. Meet younger people, talk with them. Their active enthusiasm is contagious.
5. Do more physical activities. When he's tired, he'll enjoy his comforts at home more than ever.

Pretenders

The male ego gets in the way—he wants to be viewed as a stud. In fact, he might be impotent, but that's not what he tells his friends. The last thing some men want is more sex, since they can't handle what they have at home. A woman, however, will interpret lack of sex interest as not being wanted. She will see herself as undesirable, or believe that he just prefers other women.

Your husband may avoid sex with you because his sexual desire has declined. Never tell your friends—not ever— about his diminished sex drive. You would be betraying his confidence. Instead, tell him that you have been very tired of late and ask him for abstinence until you recover. If he spends more time with you, you'll know his sex drive has declined.

He Is Easy

Your husband remembers the days when women could get all the sex they wanted and he had to be grateful for sex. One of your husband's fantasies is to have a woman seduce him. He has little resistance to a proposition.

If he was unpopular and spent most of his youth in a perpetual state of horniness, he'll welcome seduction now just for the fulfillment of a fantasy. If he was popular and had a fair share of women, he has some resistance. If he had few sexual needs or had all the sex he wanted, his resistance is high. Listen carefully to his sexual history so you'll know his tolerance for seduction.

HE DOES NOT ALWAYS WANT DIVORCE

Your husband might really care about you. Perhaps he knows he can't cope without you and that his career would suffer. The other woman might fear marriage would diminish their romance. Don't jump to the conclusion that he wants a divorce. If he did, he probably would have asked for it.

PLANNING YOUR RESPONSES

When you started dating your husband, you may have felt thrilled, but you kept your excitement from him. If he knew just how dazzled you were with him, it would have diminished his esteem for you. You knew then that you couldn't appear crazy over him, so you overcame your feelings long enough to achieve your goal. Back then you had self-control. You can have it again. This time, put aside anger long enough to have the conversations that will lead to what you want.

Letting on

Some women think it's a disadvantage to admit they know about the other woman. They think it prudent to ignore the existence of a mistress because that way, the man tries to keep "the other woman" a secret. Keep in mind that the stress of secrecy eventually makes the other woman miserable. She will reach a point where she will want to live openly with her lover and do the things people normally do in public. This tactic may backfire because the excitement and intensity of their delicious secret may enhance their romance if she has reasons for secrecy, too.

It's usually better to acknowledge you have a competitor, (first using the strategy outlined on page 67), especially if she is more than a casual fling. Never allow your intelligence to be insulted, but approach his affair without a battle. Words such as, "I believe that there's another woman in your life. I promise, I won't fight you, but don't abuse the trust I have in you. Is that the situation?" This may open communications and you may feel like leaving and never speaking to your husband again. But if you want him, you can't afford to lose contact.

If He Tells You

A distinct minority of men tell their wives that they are having sex with someone else. These are five reasons why men tell on themselves:

1. *Power*. He thinks, "What can she do about it?"
2. *Guilt*. His conscience bothers him.
3. *Responsive*. His wife is having sex with someone.
4. *Sexual*. He believes he has a right to have sex.
5. *Truthfulness*. Honesty at all costs is his motto.

Sexual Strategies

Rarely will your husband stop having sex with you because he's unfaithful. In fact, the other woman fears his lingering feelings could explode into a passion for you. As long as you have his body, but she has his heart, you can prevail. Keep your sex life active and let her know your love relationship is not dead. If you have rejected him sexually, he's learned not to approach you and you may have to seduce him.

Do not diminish his sexuality with comments about his lack of prowess. If he is sexually inadequate, he might leave you because he feels he is a failure, and will go to another woman just because he needs to be appreciated. If you can, tell him he's terrific after every sexual encounter.

Responsibility and Values

Responsibilities are important to most men. Don't be afraid to say, "You have the responsibility to . . ." He has an accountability that can't be ignored. He likes to be needed, which he equates with love.

If he is acting against his usual values by seeing another woman, focus on his self-respect. Ask him how long he can be happy when he knows he's doing the wrong thing. Point out that, with as much conflict as exists between his actions and values, his probability of happiness is slim.

COMMUNICATING

You really don't want to know that your husband is having a joyous time with the other woman, and you certainly don't want to discover how attractive or talented she is. Nevertheless, you have to go through this process to know what you're facing and to get him to doubt the wisdom of what he is doing. Without condoning the relationship, encourage him to talk. He will reveal things about her that you can later use.

Listen first, think about the specifics, and then develop your own strategy. Communication means listening—the hard part—and talking, which is the easy part. There is no prize for talking first. When your husband is cheating, there isn't a two-way street between you and him because he wants to keep silent about his actions. Your husband and the other woman reveal everything to each other. If you don't continue to communicate with your husband she keeps the advantage.

The one thing he will tell you about is his marital discontent. Ask him about his anger and grievances against you, real or imagined. Don't cut him off. Listen to things that have bothered him all along—especially to those things he never complained about. If you want him, he can be helped back to wanting you again.

HOW TO CONFRONT HIM

If your husband has affection for you, he hates lying to you. When you confront him, set the circumstances so that he feels maximum discomfort if he lies to you. Bring up a sentimental subject. When your conversation is filled with fond images, ask the question that you've wanted to ask all along. "Honey, where did you really go last Saturday afternoon?"

Don't necessarily expect your husband to answer truthfully. You may have to interpret his reaction to your question. Does he stutter or look away? Does he become belligerent, or compassionate and reassuring? Even if he won't admit that he wandered, he could feel such strong conflicts that he'll vow never to cheat again.

Alternatively, plan a long conversation. Drive into the country where you'll be together and he can't avoid you. Test his honesty with questions you already know the answers to. Then ask if he has been cheating. He may be caught off guard. If he lies, his tone of voice will change. This is an all-or-nothing gamble. If he is able to lie, he will be twice as careful from now on. Don't talk in an accusing tone because you won't get the truth that way. "I love you, and we can work this out," is a better attitude.

Your husband is likely to be misleading the other woman with stories that are only partially true, especially about you. He doesn't talk about your good times or your last passionate encounter. Tell him that he misleads her and she doesn't know him as he really is. Let him know that while you fully accept him, she may not.

If he is too self-assured, criticize him (over and above normal). Because these are harsh words, deliver them with a gentle rather than a hostile tone. Tell him that there are embarrassing moments in his past, that he isn't as smart as she thinks he is, that he has potential impotence problems, that he has lost his youth and isn't what he was. Then tell him that you know these facts and still love him. Ask him what her reactions will be when she finds out his hidden faults. Create realistic expectations by destroying any illusions of a perfect love affair.

Focus on the hassles of rearranging his life—people, prospects, lifestyle. Discussing divorce stirs up many contradictory feelings, and he may experience heavy guilt because you didn't cause the problem.

USING HIS EMOTIONS

Here are several reactions that should keep you solidly in his life. These strategies appeal to his sense of justice. Since virtually every man tries to act in a fair manner toward a woman who loves him, you should be successful.

You Need Time

Tell him that when two people have loved each other as much as you two have, it's cruel to suddenly end that closeness and shared intimacy. Just as it took time to grow as closely together as you have, you'll need time to grow apart. Even if he's not going to be your major love interest, tell him you must still see him, hold him, share your thoughts with him, and slowly end your sexual life with him. Usually a man responds to being needed, as long as that need is not all-consuming.

You Need Help

Tell him that he has dashed your expectations of life with him and that he should help to reconstruct a new life without him. Ask to be introduced to the good single men he knows. Emphasize many men will welcome his introduction since a good woman is hard to find.

Gather as much confidence as you can and be as happy as possible when you're in public with him. In private, admit that while you seem to be in good spirits and having great fun when you're out, only the two of you acknowledge your hidden sadness. It will be difficult for him not to feel some sense of possession as other men look at you with interest.

You Need Sex

Ask him to take care of your sexual needs, at least until you've found a safe and enjoyable new partner. It's scary and potentially lethal to have casual sex, and yet you need a source of gratification.

You Need His Friendship

Emphasize that a man like him is almost impossible to find. Finding a sexual partner is one thing, and eventually you're willing to give up that aspect of your relationship, but not the friendship. You want to speak to him whenever you need his ideas or input. Promise to befriend her as soon as you can control yourself enough to do so. Mention that you won't destroy any closeness with his family. He'll understand that you'll be very friendly with his parents and will take the kids over more frequently than before.

You Need Money

He may give her up if you start to talk seriously about your finances. If you and your husband have children, emphasize his personal obligations. Tell him that children should have minimum disruption in their everyday lives, that they love their father and don't want to lose him.

Then talk about financial obligations. Tell him that adultery might lead to divorce, and divorce means the income and property must be split. Discuss the standard of living the children need and what it will cost. Be very specific. Ask him what he will do about school, lessons, medical and dental expenses, allowances, birthdays, and vacations. In addition, let him know he will have to pay for psychological counseling, an accountant, and lawyers—your expenses as well as his. The cost of a settlement shocks many men into reality. He'll have to use his paycheck for child support. Your ex-husband will need the other woman's income—he had better ask if she can afford him.

The cost of your children is a potential financial disaster if he marries his mistress. If you're sure he won't do it, suggest that he get custody. If he is looking to avoid responsibility, this commitment could finish off the affair.

USE HIS FEARS

Your husband is thinking more about himself than he is about you. Increase his fears and tell him what is going to go wrong because of his adulterous relationship.

Embarrassment

Your husband fears humiliation if his adultery becomes known. Tell him his behavior is an admission to the world that he has character flaws that make him a risky partner in marriage and business.

Family Instability

Tell him that his parents resent adultery, especially if you have children. His parents will be afraid of losing their close contact to the grandchildren and will worry about the young ones losing the protection of their father.

Financial Insecurity

Tell him that his boss may doubt his dedication to the job if the boss views adultery as disloyalty.

Her Sexual Inadequacy

Point out to your husband that he may feel content now because he has two women satisfying him, and he may even seek a replacement for you should you break up, if the other woman can't meet his needs. It's one thing for her to tolerate the wife, but she won't tolerate another woman.

His Sexual Inadequacy

Point out to your husband that she might be too much woman for him.

Lack of Religious Acceptance

His church may reject him if it views adultery askance. If his membership is important to him, warn him that he may lose his contacts.

Insecure Future

You are probably his best friend. Ask him if he's thought of losing you as such. When he cheats on you he can't expect to rely on you.

Custody

If his cheating results in your separation, the children will be with you. Let him know that courts are biased in favor of women. Judges don't look favorably at placing children with husbands when there is another woman. Get clippings of stories from newspapers and magazines about what happens to fathers in custody fights.

USING HIS GUILT

Remember: He will feel guilty about what he is doing to you. Nurture this guilt with these specifics:

When Mother's Day comes, the children get you a loving card addressed to "the best mother ever." Frame the card and display it proudly and prominently.

Tell him that being his wife and the mother of his children

is the most important part of your life. Your career is important because it enhances your marriage.

Use pictures. Take your favorite photo of the family and have it enlarge to display in your living room. Have snapshots or albums conveniently around the house that can bring back fond memories. When the children's school pictures arrive, put all of them into one large frame.

HIS DIVORCE REALITIES

If your husband is still cheating, let him know the facts of life when it comes to adultery and divorce. Adultery is not free love. More often than not, the husband ends up paying more in attorney's fees, child support, and alimony when he has been cheating.

Men have naive views of marriage and divorce. Here are the ten most common wrong ideas:

1. "I can have secret assets. She can't discover what I did with them." Your attorney and investigator can uncover his assets.
2. "I did all the work, and I am entitled to everything. At best, I gave her room and board." You gave up your youth, career, and/or education. That's worth money.
3. "Adultery doesn't count, so why expend the effort to keep faithful." Adultery can count.
4. "The property is all in my name, so it's mine." That used to be the law, but it isn't true in most jurisdictions anymore.
5. "I can hide." There are new laws that help you find him.

6. "This divorce is simple, it's no-fault." Not so when there are assets or children, or it is contested. It can take years.

7. "We are going our separate ways." Any change in financial circumstances brings you back to court. Inflation alone will require adjustments in support.

8. "I'll make child support payments and that's the end of it." Not so; your child's extraordinary expenses are an ex-husband's responsibility, too.

9. "She's to blame." If he's having an affair, it's his responsibility, not yours.

10. "She doesn't have money to fight me." You don't have to have money. The court will award you attorney's fees and he'll have to pay them.

4

WHAT ABOUT ME?

When a woman discovers that her husband is cheating, her first thought is, "It can't be true." She believes her marriage is stronger than others. But when she realizes the truth—that her husband is seeing another woman—she is hurt more than she thought she could be hurt by anything. Her pride is shattered. She becomes angry, and she wants revenge.

Act in your best interest instead of getting revenge. Your crucial task now is controlling yourself long enough to let your true feelings surface. Until you can rationally face your dilemma—and you'll know that is happening when you can balance the good times against the bad—don't decide your future. Put your marriage on "automatic pilot." Grant your husband a grace period to come to his senses. Retreat from the firing line until you assess your artillery.

You may believe that you have failed if your husband

cheats, but do not blame yourself. Most important, do not think that you could have stopped him, and do not spend months agonizing over each moment in your life.

These are tough times; you must toughen up to succeed. With the proper perspective, you can come to your senses rather quickly. You will get all kinds of help from many sources. Even strangers will help you. Controlling your feelings will be possible because your friends will gladly help you cope.

YOUR ANGER

Your fury at your husband is perhaps the most negative emotion you have ever experienced. If you understand your feelings, you can better evaluate what you really want to do. Here are some ideas that can help you cope with your anger and resolve your course of action.

It's Your Right

You have a *right* to be angry. Once you assert this, you free yourself from blame. It's not your fault.

Plan Your Attack

Look at your anger as a huge lump, then consider whether you should swallow it or cut it in pieces. It's better that you should savor each morsel.

Don't Tell Him

Do not let him know what you are thinking until you formulate your plan. Keep that advantage.

You're Normal

Your anger is a normal reaction to cheating. The angrier you are, the more intense the love you have for your mate.

Your Fury

When you are ready, let your mate know how furious you are. Getting even won't help you. If you insist on doing something nasty, do it without scaring him away forever.

Revealing your hurt, anger, and shock is usually enough to start the mending process.

Reap Benefits

Reap benefits from your anger. When you're angry, you have thoughts such as, "If I had known, I would never have allowed myself to be in this position," or "I should just chuck it all." You are experiencing enormous bursts of emotions and thoughts. Write down your ideas, because they can help you formulate new attitudes, which in turn can strengthen you and your relationship. You probably haven't focused on yourself and your needs in a long time. Anger redirects your attention to yourself and keeps you from being a wimp.

Be Courageous

Anger gives you the courage to speak the whole truth. If controlled, it can help you vent grievances. You didn't always tell your mate what was on your mind because at the time it could have hurt his feelings. When you're angry, you're not concerned about his feelings.

Make Up

Anger releases your pent-up frustrations and makes room for positive feelings. If you make up, your love life can be better than ever.

Talk

Verbalize all your frustrations to make room for the good feelings you may have for your husband.

Take Control

Use time to your advantage. If he wants to go slowly you can hurry. You know his patience level and how to frustrate his plans. Evaluate your circumstances when you're in control. Not every relationship is worth saving, but yours might be. Before you make a decision you may have to live with for the rest of your life, cool off.

ANGER ISN'T FOREVER

Some anger will continue while some will fade away. How long will yours last? Is there a peak? Have you already reached it? Does anger continue forever, or does it eventually diminish? Can you control it? What can you do to get rid of it?

Suppose you were alone for one single day with no phone, radio, or television. During this twenty-four hours, how much time would you spend thinking of your mate? At first, your anger will grow as the hours pass. But later, maybe much later, it will start to subside. You don't have to spend time alone to recognize that anger isn't forever. Give yourself time.

DEALING WITH YOUR ANGER
TOWARD HIM

One or more of these ideas can help you overcome your anger so that you can deal with your husband.

Motivate Yourself

Push yourself to regain self-control. If you can't manage yourself, you can't expect to influence him and change your circumstances.

See Him

Until you're sure you don't want him, see him at least once a week. Have a friendly and sexual encounter, if possible. If you ignore him, he's left alone, and he's openly available to the other woman.

Be Compassionate

You're kind to strangers. He expects you'll treat him with compassion if you really love him. It's foolish to have consideration for everyone but him.

Give Him a Chance to Repent

He lied to spare your feelings and keep your relationship intact and may deeply regret his actions. A repentant man often stays true after he realizes the jeopardy to his marriage.

Sex Doesn't Mean Love

Many men are polygamous. His wandering, especially if he didn't plan it, may hurt your ego, but it isn't necessarily a reflection of any lack of love for you. Women usually wander if they feel passion for a new lover, and not just out of idle curiosity, as men do.

His Buddies

Your husband has outside pressures. Male friends ridicule him if a woman offers sex and he refuses. And while women aren't encouraged to accept sexual opportunities, men are often stigmatized if they refuse a woman's sexual advances.

His Sex Drive

When a man gets sexually aroused, he wants immediate satisfaction. Under these circumstances, a woman means relief, not love.

Be Mature

If you whine too long, you'll start looking childish to him. Immaturity is not the way to win him back or to strengthen yourself.

Indulge Yourself

Pamper yourself with favorite activities; keep a smile on your face and some sparkle in your eyes. Any happiness you can show makes you incredibly attractive, especially if he's remorseful.

Let Him Vent

If all else fails, ask him to sit down with you for twenty minutes, during which time you vent all your anger. Sometimes you can forgive after you've told him off.

COPING

Crying

Nothing shows sadness like tears swelling in your eyes. Your crying touches your husband's conscience, especially when he is the cause of your sorrow. If you cry too easily, or too often, he'll think you're immature. Let him see you sob when the bad moments are intense, but avoid weeping and whining.

Get Sympathy

Although they can be as devastating as a physical injury, emotional wounds are very private. Revealing that your feelings have been severely hurt is embarrassing. You weren't hurt accidentally. Your husband, the closest person to you and the one who has given you much joy, is the person who is creating this pain. Yet, you can't get sympathy unless you tell others.

You're suffering from deep anguish but you can lessen anguish if you confide in your friends. Treat your distress in the same manner as you would treat a physical problem. If you broke your leg, your friends would sign the cast with affectionate messages.

Analyze Your False Pride

Imagine yourself living on a deserted island with your husband. You can do exactly as you wish because you don't have to explain your actions to anyone—no probing questions to answer, no snoopy neighbors, no one to say "you should" or "you shouldn't," or tell you how they would handle the situation. What then would your feelings be toward your husband?

How much of your concern about his adultery is really based on what others will say, or how others will react to you, or how foolish you may appear if you don't demand some sort of public retribution? You may decide that something within you could never recover from the hurt of a cheating husband, but it's *your* reaction, no one elses.

SEX AS A SPORT

What makes men so different from women? Some men enjoy sexual variety and are inclined to have an affair if there are no consequences. The man's ideal self-image is that of a great lover and not that of a family man. Consider that there are no men's publications called *Working Father* or *Family Fidelity.*

For some men, sex is just another physical activity, such as tennis or golf. The person he has sex with could be as significant to him as his last game. He thinks that you, the woman he loves, provides for, and shares his life with, shouldn't be concerned because he had a half-hour tryst with someone he barely remembers.

REVISING THE DOUBLE STANDARD

You would think that men who view casual sex as non-threatening to a committed relationship would apply the same reasoning if their women had casual affairs. They don't. There's a double standard because sex is a romantic venture for women and there is a risk of pregnancy.

For you, sex is not a casual event. You feel affection for your husband and include it as a part of sex. Women understand that a man can separate sex and love, yet women are deeply hurt if their mates wander. A woman believes the "other woman" is being romanced, whether she is or not. Look to the surrounding circumstances to see if sex with another woman is seriously displacing you in his heart.

TYPES OF AFFAIRS

If your mate's fling was unplanned, try to apply male standards to his action. Attribute it to his weakness. He might have been caught up in the spirit of the moment, or the woman might have surprised him with an offer for a sexual encounter.

If the encounters are planned, then he's romanticizing the affair. He cares for the other woman as a person. He is not separating sex and affection because he is concerned about *her* feelings. In this case, she's a real threat to you.

Whether it's a fling or a serious affair, look to the number of encounters. When curiosity is the primary feeling a man has toward his sex partner, it's very difficult to sustain sexual interest for more than a dozen trysts with that person. If, after a dozen meetings, he looks forward with enthusiasm to seeing her, then he's sharing more than sexual passions with her.

Your mate thinks he can love both of you. Under these circumstances, he may act in a very strange way to resolve his dilemma. He may set himself up to be caught. Be prepared for the showdown between you and the other woman. He may test which one loves him more by condoning his actions, wanting and forgiving him. He may need to test himself to see how he would choose.

CHOOSING AN ALLY

You need an ally—someone close by who can help you through your difficult times. She is going to influence you in a major decision that will affect your happiness for life. Don't give just anyone that privilege. Choose someone who is smart and prudent. Consider these essential prerequisites. Your ally should be:

A Listener

You need to verbalize your every thought. By expressing yourself fully, it's easier for her to know what you want. Listening to yourself under the guise of speaking to her is a great help.

A Prejudiced Ally

Your ally's job is to be your advocate, so she should know about your goals. Make sure that she isn't out for herself.

A Contemporary

Only someone in your generation knows exactly how the world will treat you and what you can realistically expect. She should know what's awaiting you in social and economic contexts.

An "Expendable" Person

When your marital crisis is resolved, her presence may remind you of your many painful experiences. You'll avoid her as long as you're sensitive to your crisis. If it takes a long time to heal the memories, your friendship will fade.

A Happy Person

Advice from an unhappy person is risky. If your ally couldn't arrange a joyful existence for herself, it's even less likely she can guide you to happiness.

APPEASEMENT

Think about your fears of adultery. Would you condone his adultery under any of these circumstances?

1. He has never put your marriage in jeopardy and he doesn't believe in divorce.
2. His flings are casual.
3. You're his number-one love.
4. He's home every night, holidays and weekends.

5. He is very discreet and sees other women only if he's out of town.
6. He doesn't spend money on the other woman.
7. He's very careful and always uses condoms if he's with another woman. He never risks AIDS or pregnancy.
8. He never puts his income or career at risk.
9. He feels so guilty he always buys you an expensive gift.
10. A good provider, he gives you all the money he earns.

Would any of these circumstances help you forgive him or accept the affair?

THE FAITHFUL SCOUNDREL AND THE EXEMPLARY CHEATER

How important is fidelity to you now? Is adultery unforgivable? Before answering this question, consider two hypothetical men:

1. *The faithful scoundrel.* He gambles, drinks, borrows money from you, and sells your car, but he doesn't have sex with anyone but you.
2. *The exemplary cheater.* He doesn't do anything wrong, except one thing. He has sex with someone else.

If you had to choose one of these two individuals, which would you pick? Would other actions upset you just as much as finding a lover? Suppose he:

1. gambles his paycheck.
2. pawns your engagement ring.

3. changes his religion.
4. sells "his" house without your knowledge.
5. invests everything in a losing business venture.
6. has sex with a woman he does not know.
7. has sex with his ex-wife.
8. snubs your parents.
9. ignores his children.
10. admits to being bisexual.

Which of these could you forgive? It seems illogical to forgive many other "heinous" actions, but still hold adultery to be unforgivable.

MITIGATING CIRCUMSTANCES

Suppose there are actually benefits to you if he sees the other woman. Would it matter less to you? Here are some situations that other women face.

1. She's his boss. She gets him promotions and good assignments.
2. She holds the mortgage on your house. When you've missed payments, she has been very understanding and accepted very late checks.
3. She is a rich older woman. Your husband will inherit her home, business, and cash.
4. She's given your husband money for the children's tuition on several occasions.
5. In her own way, she has the highest regards for you and the family. She insists your husband be responsible to you and doesn't want him divorced.

I haven't made up these situations. In some cases, the wife understood and accepted the circumstances. In others, the wife's furor was greater. What matters is *your* reaction to these circumstances.

Polygamy

Our society's reactions to polygamy are based upon how we are taught we should treat our mates, not on our own desires or needs. In some societies, men have several wives who coexist as sister-wives and share responsibilities. Those of us who do not understand their harmony ask ourselves, how can these women gleefully share one man? The sister-wives think we're missing out by not having other women sharing the household duties. What you were taught may not be what's best for you. Think of your own needs first.

Terminal Illness

If your husband were terminally ill, would you encourage him to go on a hedonistic binge and do all the living he ever wanted to do? Suppose you were ill? Would you free him to start seeking companionship elsewhere?

If you understand, even condone, adultery under certain conditions, at least you realize that there are degrees of guilt—you would forgive certain situations. Perhaps you can extend your forgiving nature to your own special circumstances.

FIND A MIDDLE GROUND

Some women treat their husbands as if committing adultery is the ultimate evil. Even if they oppose capital punishment, they would do dire things to their husbands. They speak of killing, castration, divorce, and some other things that good taste requires I don't mention.

At the other extreme, many women ignore their husbands' adultery. Especially if the relationship does not embarrass the family, their attitude is, "business as usual." There could be some saber-rattling, but the wife isn't going to do anything about it.

Can a woman oppose her husband's adultery, but in moderation? Is there a middle ground? You wouldn't walk away or ignore other major problems; this one is no different. The plan of action that brings you the result you want is your middle ground. Dedicating a few minutes a day to your problems will give you the effective plan of action.

What Do You Say When You Find Out?

Discourage his further involvement with the other woman. "Please don't. I love you too much and I can't stop loving you," should put a real damper on his good times with her. Be cautious, but continue the relationship. "I won't precipitate events. I won't kick you out. I won't take you away from your kids. I will give you continuous love." These are the ideas you want to convey to him and he will pass them on to her. That will upset her even more than she upsets you.

Create a Hiatus

You need a yellow caution light for your feelings and where they're heading. Think of how you fell in love. It took time. Falling out of love also takes time. Spending time with him is your only way to know whether you want to go ahead or stop.

Since this is a hiatus, become aware of other men. Lessen your dependency on your mate and seek the companionship of others. Since you've been in a long, exclusive relationship, you need new conversational outlets.

Should I Sleep with Him?

For your own sake, continue your sex life with your husband. If you ignore your sexual needs, you are punishing yourself. No matter how angry you are at him, as your sexual desire increases, you will think about him more.

Improve Your Skills

At the same time, brush up your skills in attracting and talking to men. Start conversations with men you're not attracted to but who are pleasant. It's too difficult to start talking with men if you're worried about being liked.

Once you're skilled at starting conversations, then seek men you're attracted to. Some men enjoy being the aggressor, still they only approach a friendly woman such as you. You can always say no tactfully if you don't want him.

Spend some time every day enjoying yourself. Just be sure it's fun. Do simple things such as listening to favorite music, joining an exercise class, puttering with your plants, or gossiping with friends. These distractions will help you stop thinking about your husband. Have fun or you will start looking like a sourpuss.

Do something that you've always wanted to do but were too lazy to start. This is your time to take an enrichment course, go on a weekend trip with friends, upgrade your wardrobe, get a new hairdo, or join a country club. If you improve your self-image, he will start wanting you again. At the very least, he will be curious about the new you.

Deal with Your Uncertainty

Regardless of what decision you make, you will anguish over whether you're doing the right thing. No matter how angry you are at your husband, you remember the good times. If you revive your relationship, you remember the bad times.

Since you are uncertain, openly talk about it with your friends. No one is going to listen endlessly, but a friend will give you an hour. Call her up and say, "I'd like to talk to you over lunch—I need a good listener." When you express your doubts, it helps you firm your final decision. Sometimes, you will be able to tell by your friends' reactions that your doubts are normal. You're not the only one who's been in a dilemma. A worse situation for you would be to not decide your own fate.

Ask yourself, can the grief caused by your mate have a happy resolution? Can your relationship be revitalized and fun again, not just saved? Is it worth the effort? If so, how? Are you better off hanging on or letting go? Alone again—is that what you want?

Ask yourself questions about your relationship in an organized manner. A good strategy is to assume that you are evaluating the situation for your twin sister, who is identical to you in every respect except that she has *not* suffered the mental anguish you have suffered with your mate. Would he be good for her?

To keep your love alive requires moments of fun every day and evidence of those qualities that made you intriguing to each other in the first place. It may seem unfair that the happiness of yesterday is so quickly forgotten and that grief seems to last forever. The fun of yesterday matters little; it's the joys of today that count.

Recognize the Shift of Power

Odds shift in the man's favor in time. He doesn't know how valuable he has become until he discovers women will chase him. A woman who wouldn't smile at him in her youth now wants to date him. If he's more than ordinary, the more he will be desired by his female peers and younger women. You should take this into account. Since he's older, even if he has less hair and a potbelly, he's more desirable than ever. There are likable things about him. Think twice before letting him go—you're throwing away a relationship that ultimately may be your last.

You may fantasize that your past boyfriends would flock to your side if you were available. Maybe you are right, but make sure. Call a few old flames to see how happy they are to hear from you. Realistic expectations make for right decisions.

Make Future Plans

You could increase bonding with your husband by actively planning for the future. If you treat your future together as a bond, invest time, money, and effort in it.

A happy marriage is based on happiness in the past, present, and particularly the future. Your early days were some of your best because you contemplated a happy future. Don't stop planning one now just because you've lived a good part of your life. There's always something new to see or experience.

You and your husband are in a lifeboat, rowing together against the tides. If he endangers the lifeboat through his infidelity, your reaction shouldn't be to put bigger holes in the hull. Fight with him in private, but stand with him against the world.

5

THE BITCH

When there's another woman threatening your marriage, more likely than not you can prevail. If you want your husband and are willing to put even more effort into the relationship, face the competition and start fighting back.

You can defeat the other woman if you know about her and know what strategies you can use against her. Then, you can easily invade her life (even if she is his ex-wife).

Once, you were romantically the most important person in your husband's life—the one for whom he gave up his bachelorhood. You had him to yourself for a long time, and that exclusivity can be achieved again. There are situations you can create and circumstances that will help.

YOUR COMPETITION

Your husband can cheat almost anywhere, but there is a higher probability with certain women. If you know your competition you can ward them off.

His Ex-wife

Your husband's liaison with his ex-wife is dangerous if he has any feelings for her left over from the marriage. Hatred or anger is a passion, and these persistent emotions can explode into sexual desire.

His Ideal

She is the woman your husband dreamed of but never met. You can find out his image of an ideal mate just by asking him. If he has always talked about a five foot, two inch redhead with a smattering of freckles on her nose who loves football and math, beware if she appears.

The One That Got Away

If your husband wanted someone, but couldn't get her, his desire for her may continue until he realizes she wasn't so special after all.

Your Neighbor

Proximity can create curiosity. If your husband sees your neighbor consistently, he may wonder what she's like sexually.

Family Members

Even if she is your relative, that's no guarantee your husband will feel brotherly toward her. In fact, your female relatives may have many of the qualities that make you attractive to your husband.

Exotic Women

Your husband may be curious about a type of woman who is different from you. He may seek her to satisfy his curiosity about another culture.

Co-workers

Your husband spends as much time with his co-workers as he does with you when you're awake. It's natural for him to bond with people who share his work experiences.

Salespeople and Waitresses

He interacts with these women on a continuing basis. Just ask a waitress how often she's asked for a date!

Schoolmates

A class reunion may seem an unlikely place for your husband to be tempted, but if he discovers that a girl he was attracted to also secretly liked him, he may decide to have a little fling with her.

Caregivers

Men are attracted to women who are in nurturing professions. They assume that women who provide for people's needs are kindly. When your husband sees the care and patience a nurse displays toward his father, it occurs to him that he would enjoy it, too.

Some of the women mentioned are greater threats than others. The ex-wife, co-worker, and his heartthrob require specific strategies; with the others, your presence is usually deterrent enough.

IF THE OTHER WOMAN IS HIS EX-WIFE

The most dangerous "other woman" you face may be your husband's ex-wife. She has many circumstances in her favor:

1. She is the mother of his children.
2. He did love her once.
3. She is comfortable with him because he knows her well.
4. They share some good memories.
5. They had a sexual bond.

In some situations, his ex-wife can be your closest ally. Marriage didn't work out for them before; it's not going to work out now. She may recognize that your husband is not her ideal mate and be delighted he's with you.

Before you decide whether she's a friend or foe, consider five crucial aspects of your husband's relationship with his ex-wife that now have a residual impact on you: their past relationship itself, the children, present circumstances, nostalgia, and comparisons with your relationship now. Evaluate these factors for yourself.

Their Past Relationship

How did your husband's relationship with his ex-wife end? If it's still simmering, be prepared. His renewed interest in her could get it to boil over. If it ended, but you didn't cause the breakup, he'll prefer you. But if you separated them, they might try to patch things up.

The Children

Did your husband live with his ex-wife during their children's formative years? If a man believes that your relationship is thwarting his paternal instinct, he might turn emotionally to his ex-wife. He might miss the "familyness" of the children— their activities and achievements. If so, he will think of her.

Always speak about his children as "our responsibility" and delight in their successes. Mention often that you are looking forward to grandchildren someday and you expect him to be a doting grandfather. Fuss at him if he ignores his kids.

Present Circumstances

Things change, but the more they do, the more they affect your husband and his ex-wife. If she became impoverished, he might help her. If she became a movie star, he might want to be with her. If she became an important official, he might want to be with her at the citadel of power. Is she more desirable now than when they were married?

Nostalgia

Nostalgia can be important. When he and his ex-wife were together, he might have been athletic, handsome, well-respected, and wealthy. Now he has become sedentary and less than handsome—an ordinary person trying to make a living. She remembers how he used to be. Even if he didn't achieve his goals, at least he remembers his best time. If he and his ex-wife were together during the prime of his life, he may think of her when he thinks of the good old days.

Relationships Compared

Some of the problems you're solving now are similar to the problems his ex-wife solved in the past. If so, he is likely to think of her and how she handled similar situations. He may prefer her solutions to yours. You can't stop his comparisons, but you can involve him more in solving the problems.

STRATEGIES YOU CAN USE

His Ex-Wife

Your husband might miss his ex-wife. In the worst of divorces, the couple remembers with fondness certain people, places, and things. Your husband may miss the way his ex-wife fluffed the pillows, or even her systematic squeezing of the toothpaste tube. Don't be alarmed if he speaks of his ex-wife with fondness, as long as it's not all the time. Remember, he also misses his mother.

He once did love her. He might even think he left her with a right of first refusal. If his ex-wife wants him back, be prepared for some desire on his part, regardless of the circumstances. Many men who are faithful to their wives will have sex with their ex-wives. They believe that it is just a continuation of their relationship, though interrupted by events such as your marriage.

Encourage your mate to talk about the highlights of his past marriage, then express your sympathy that he and his former wife couldn't succeed as a couple. If he has intense feelings for his ex-wife, even hate, then praise her. He will then remember her nastiness. The more he relives the past, the less intense it becomes. Eventually, he will reach indifference about his ex-wife, and that's what you want.

His Co-worker

The other woman often works in your husband's business. She has the proximity to celebrate his little joys and cushion his bad news. She easily becomes indispensable to him. Don't allow any other woman that exclusive privilege.

Treat his business cares as classified information. Learn about his company's business cycle, his industry problems, and his competitors, as well as his boss and secretary and co-workers.

The more attention you pay to his business concerns, the more important you become to him.

His Heartthrob

In virtually every man's life, there was a woman he wanted, but loved and lost. A fond memory, one day she reappears in his life.

The heartthrob poses a real danger to your marital fidelity because your husband's affection, and curiosity as to her life, has been simmering for a long time.

Diffuse some of her mystique by inviting her over to your home. Ask about her health, her romantic life, her disappointments, her family and obligations. Once your husband hears the story of her life, she becomes less than the perfect image he carries of her. If possible, you want your husband

110

to conclude that she's become an ordinary person. The less mystique, the less extraordinary she becomes.

Show her that your home is a happy one, which should put a damper on any thoughts she might have of a romantic future with your husband. Especially with her, rarely use the pronoun *I*. Always use *we*. Refer to yourself as if you and your husband are an inseparable team.

A few don'ts:

1. Don't bring out your wedding album. She might think that it was your last happy occasion! Instead, show recent pictures of you both.
2. Don't reveal any of your husband's faults or weaknesses. Brag about him. She'll attribute your oversights of his frailties to love.
3. If she asks you about yourself, answer and turn the conversation back to her. You want *her* mystique eroded.
4. Don't worry about being the perfect hostess. Don't be serving while your husband and she can talk freely alone. Any friendship or bonding that could form should include you.

You can capture any affection your husband felt for her by using transference. It's easy to achieve if you let him talk freely about her. Ask him the questions about her that you're thinking. He will talk about her because he thinks "it is just in the past."

1. How much did he want her?
2. Did he ever tell her his feelings?
3. How intimidated was he by her?
4. What was his fantasy with her?
5. How often did he see her?

6. Did she ever show interest in him?
7. What did he like most about her?
8. Did she have other boyfriends?
9. Why didn't he look her up?
10. Is she much the same now as she was then?

YOUR WEAPONS

If you don't know who she is, you probably think about the other woman more than you'd care to admit. You imagine she is young and beautiful, and that she has a vibrant personality and a good figure. In your fantasy, she's lively and energetic (after all, most likely she doesn't have a husband and children to care for), carefree and fun.

Don't let her intimidate you. If she's so wonderful, why haven't available men flocked to her? She would probably trade places with you if she could. Would you trade places with her?

In reality, the other woman comes in all shapes and sizes and a variety of ages. In fact, a group of other women doesn't look much different from a group of wives.

Time

Time is on your side. The other woman is waiting for him, but her clock is ticking. She's aware that relationships peak, plateau, and sometimes fizzle out. His incentive to leave you and marry her decreases with time. Then he'll be afraid to marry her since his feelings aren't as strong.

The uncertainty of when he will be free magnifies all the other uncertainties in her life. The longer she waits, the more desperate she becomes. Will he become available? If she's waiting for the right time and circumstances, it may never happen. She wonders if he's strong enough to leave you. Their biggest bond is their weakness. She understands his cowardliness because she's a wimp, too.

Secrecy Hurts Her

The other woman has many desperate and lonely moments. Her own family won't listen to her. In their view, at best she's a fool, at worst an immoral home wrecker. Only a few friends can share her secret. She keeps these friends on a string because she can't keep appointments—your husband might show up. She doesn't want to admit to her friends that her love interest is someone else's man. She is frustrated by not being able to speak of him.

If her friends see her with your husband, they'll ask questions she doesn't want to answer. If his friends see them, she must act as though she doesn't know him or as though they are just casual friends. She is unnerved when they pretend in public that they don't know each other. At first, she may enjoy fooling people, but after a while, she wonders if the joke could be on her.

Her Advantage Is Temporary

For your husband, there is a thrill to newness. She has a temporary advantage because his curiosity is now on her side. But man is a creature of habit. After the initial sparkle of a new body, he misses his home, surroundings, and family. He would rather talk about his day and be with you. The greatest loss the man feels is the habit of *talking* to his wife.

Passive Acceptance

The other woman quietly waits until your husband is available; his priorities take precedence over hers. If she is aggressive, he won't put up with her behavior. She might not demand security in their relationship because she views herself as undeserving.

STRATEGIES TO USE ON HER

You can create situations that can help you take the offensive.

"Vacations"

If your husband is seeing another woman, it's possible that he just wants a short vacation from your marriage. You could ignore her existence for a while, but if it's more than a "vacation," there are a few things you could do.

If your husband and the other woman see each other only rarely, leave them together long enough that they discover they don't like each other. The isolated mountain cabin for a solitary week might destroy their relationship, since their passion continues unabated because they fantasize togetherness is bliss. Give them time for boredom.

Create situations where he would prefer to stay home. If you know he's going to see her Thursday, invite his friends over for drinks that night. If he's having dinner with her on Saturday, that's the day to make his favorite meal and invite his parents.

Destroy Her Secret Life

There is something special about sharing a secret with someone. That feeling is intense and special precisely because it is so private, so unique, to two people. Secret lovers talk about how people would react if they knew, how they were nearly caught together, their plans to continue the charade, and what would happen if they did get caught.

Their closeness is based on the fear of exposure. If they are uncovered, their fantasy ends. So, simply, expose them. Tell him you know about them and probably many others have figured it out, too.

Give Her a Chance to Bore Him

If you are open about his relationship, offer to help him. If he thinks he loves her, tell him that he should know something about the person who's captivated his attention. Give him some ideas about the questions he should ask. Suggest personal questions about her life. You know the patience your husband has to listen to her personal history. If he's like most men, he'd rather talk than listen.

Tell him not to be selfish, but to ask her about her day, her problems, her feelings, her family and friends. He should ask:

1. What was it like growing up in her hometown?
2. What's her romantic history?
3. How special is her family and who are her favorite relatives?
4. What does she expect to be doing five years from now?
5. What were the ten most important events in her life?

You want her to talk for hours. Getting these facts about her takes time. If you're lucky, he'll feel like a patient who pays for therapy but must listen to the therapist ramble about himself. He'll get fed up.

You're Favored to Win

Your husband might be fooling her. He talks with her of leaving you, but he might postpone divorce or make it indefinite, saying, "When my children are older," "When my mother passes away," or "When I secure my assets." He might not intend to end his marriage.

Basically, he wants both of you. His strategy is to promise her enough that she will continue the relationship. Her strategy is to wait until you throw him away.

Call his bluff. Create a situation where he won't leave you. You might speak about your potential pregnancy, or that you might need some medical tests. Invite his parents to visit and stay with you. She will be in anguish and doubt him when he explains that he has to be home more.

Her romantic bliss is based on infatuation. A moment of truth brings her to the reality that he won't leave you. Picture the scene: She is tearful, crying. How will he react? Probably, he'll leave her. At minimum he will have these doubts:

1. He's been through hard times with you and knows you're dependable, but is she?
2. He knows you really love him, but does she?
3. He knows the children need you and him; do they need or want her around?
4. He knows his family likes you. Will they speak to her, or to him?

If she suspects he has lingering feelings for you, she knows you'll get him back. Even if he told her your marriage is over, it's not over until you say it is. Even if he packs his bags, he'll probably return if you give him enough rope.

Family Emergencies

Emphasize family emergencies to divert his attention. Tell him you need his car, or the dog needs to be taken to a vet, or that the bathroom flooded. He'll be so concerned by your emergency that he will delay his date with her. This will make her melancholy—but that's the point.

Her anxiety increases when he is late, so create a diversion to delay their tryst. If necessary, help him find his car keys, and don't hurry.

Promises to Break

Make sure that he can't keep his small promises to her. If he can't call at six or meet her for breakfast as planned, she'll realize he can't keep the big promises, either. He hurts her when he agrees to see her but doesn't. She's feeling special and desirable and is anticipating good sex and intimate conversation. If you can postpone her party by keeping your husband at home, she will be devastated. Cancel it a few times in a row and she will start making comparisons as to who is sacrificing more. He has someone who fixes him dinner, a family to be with, people to talk to. He is not alone—she is.

She wonders whether she is a fool. She ponders, "If he can't make it for dinner in three attempts, will he ever ask for a divorce? Does he really care about me enough?" If he isn't reliable, she can't count on him.

Gradually, you can win. She'll fight you and turn into a shrew. Every doubt, every panic, every disappointment increases her frustration. She reaches the point where she must speak up or give up. Either way, you win.

If She Confronts You

If you find out about the affair in detail because she tells you about it, you may be furious, but you might be better off than you thought. Perhaps she told you because she's more afraid of a confrontation with your husband than with you. She knows he won't face you, so she's hoping you'll be furious and hurt and precipitate the divorce. She's trying to force your hand and end the marriage. Don't hand him over that easily.

Tell her she's very attractive and reminds you of several of his past girlfriends. You understand your husband's weakness; she should learn to be tolerant, too.

THINGS YOU SHOULD FIND OUT

You can increase the effectiveness of your strategies if you know certain facts about her relationship with others.

Her Romantic Record

How serious is her affair? Does she really want him or is it just a fling? Some women are mistresses by choice. She may enjoy being single, want several men in her life and complete independence. If this is so, her track record shows she won't settle down with anyone. When the time comes, tell your husband that he risks losing you and her and winding up alone.

Who's Keeping Whom?

You may think that the other woman is being financially pampered by your husband. The reality is often quite different.

Some men can justify having sex outside of marriage, but they can't justify taking food out of their children's mouths. They're unwilling to jeopardize their families' well-being by spending money on another woman. The solution is to have a relationship with a woman who's financially well-off, or at least isn't putting a financial burden on him.

Do You Know Her?

The other woman might be someone you know. She might even be someone you've viewed as a friend—at least, before you discovered the affair.

You're absolutely furious because you feel that you've been sabotaged by a friend and confidante, but her attitude may surprise you. She'll say that you "told me that you didn't want him, so I took him." She'll think you have no reason to be angry at her.

Let's look at your conversation to see why she feels that her actions are justifiable. Like most women, you confide in your female friends, not in your husband. You've been open and honest with them, telling them that your husband is lazy around the house and would rather talk politics than repair the roof; that you and he don't enjoy the same types of recreation and can never agree where to go on vacation; and that he's always after you for sex. You might even have mentioned that you reject his values and goals.

These statements, as she interprets them, show your displeasure with your husband. You might even have made her interested in him. She enjoys his high sex drive, is happy to talk about politics, and is glad to pay for roof repair. She may find his values and goals, as well as his preference for vacation and recreation, to be much to her liking.

You intended your comments to mean that you're trying hard to make your marriage work. She interpreted your statements to mean that you don't want him. In reflecting back on what has happened, you should have been more specific about your intentions.

121

Since you can talk with her, let her know that your husband will replace her, too. If you really want to be bitchy, suggest to her that your husband offered to have an active sex life with you even if he married her.

The Married Mistress

Most mistresses are single, but your husband's might be married. Even if she isn't, she might say she is. Precisely because she is unavailable and wants secrecy, men feel safe seeing her.

Your husband's big fear is a jealous husband. Use it. Television news and newspapers are filled with stories of irate husbands injuring or killing their wives' lovers. Make comments about the stories so your husband hears about the violence.

INVADING HER LIFE

The Mistress's Advantage

You could behave like a mistress, but she can't behave like you. The other woman listens intently to your husband and understands him. He's not just offering sex, he's offering the deepest intimacy of his thoughts, hopes, and fantasies. Being with her is much like therapy with sex, and all for free. He knows she won't kiss and tell; she loves him—or at least he thinks she does.

Confronting Her

It's difficult to determine when, if ever, it's advantageous to confront the other woman. Not every woman involved with a married man knows that he's married. If she discovers her lover isn't truthful, she may not continue seeing him. If so, a confrontation would help you.

Can You Find Her?

You'll need her name, address, and phone number. If you know only her name, and she has a listed telephone number, it may take hours to locate her in the directory.

If you have found the other woman, what do you want to say to her? You may have mixed feelings. You may want to call her every dirty name in the book and tell her she has a fight on her hands because you are not giving up your man, but don't threaten her with bodily harm.

Calling her names may make you feel better, but she won't stand by idly while you call her a whore. Expect her to defend herself and tell you off. She might say, "If you had been a better wife," or "If you had satisfied him more, he would not have come to me." Be ready to receive insults.

Sisterhood has its limitations. The other woman feels no

great loyalty to you. More often than not, she feels there is nothing wrong with what she's doing. Her motto is, "If it was a good marriage, he wouldn't seek another woman." If you confront the other woman, she may want your husband more.

In today's society, few people really care about the other woman. Unless you're in a very small town, you will not be able to make her the object of public ridicule by name-calling or revealing her role. A violent or vulgar confrontation with her can hurt in different ways. When your mate finds out—and she will tell him—he could be angry at you.

Praising Her

She is the enemy, but should you praise her or criticize her? Obviously, a different approach is used when you talk to your husband than when you talk to her. When speaking to him, praise her. Tell him how wonderful she is, a most marvelous person! She can't live up to that image. He will naturally think of her faults.

If you speak to her privately, demean her. Portray her as trying to take the leftovers from your life. Treat her as an also-ran, low in status. She may not leave your husband alone, but your words will depress her.

Get Him Away from Her

It may not be practical to move to the opposite end of the earth, or even to the next town, but your situation will improve if you get your husband away from his mistress.

If you can't move away, take a vacation with your husband. If you and he are on a cruise, it will be virtually impossible for him to stay in contact with her. Your next best alternative is a resort that doesn't have telephones.

The longer and more frequently you get away with your husband, the more likely you'll be able to break his bonds with her. There is some merit to the old adage, "Out of sight, out of mind."

Vacations are better than other trips because they'll prompt his mistress to think that you and your husband are enjoying your lives together and are restoring your love. When you travel with your husband, try to visit new places and see unusual things. New experiences can stimulate your rebonding.

Her Family

Since you're on the attack, contact the parents of the other woman, if you can, to help you bring their daughter to her senses. How can she explain the affair to her family? Thinking of a married man with their daughter will create sadness. Put the blame on your husband. Her family will blame her for you.

Call Her Number

Most husbands leave some means of reaching the other woman in case of family emergencies. Be sure to get a phone number where you can reach your husband. When you know he is not with her, call and be friendly with whomever answers, and then ask for your husband. The reaction of the party should give you a clue to how nonplussed she is. Whether she answers, or someone else screens your husband's calls, you've learned something (i.e., whether she has a roommate, a boyfriend, or a husband; if the number is that of her office; or if she lives with her parents).

Why You Must Fight

Your husband might be telling her only the bad side of your relationship. He may have said you're a shrew. Appear to be assertive but friendly when you talk with her. And don't cry—might be considered weakness.

The other woman might expect that you'll easily give him up. Once you show her you want him, she could withdraw. In fact, your husband probably told her that you didn't want him. Merely by going forward and expressing your case, you will show her that your husband has already deceived her.

If you have personal contact with her, or people who know her, wear a new necklace with a heart engraved "with love." Create an excuse to get your husband to travel with you overnight. If she finds out that he's bought you jewelry, or a negligee, or taken you to a motel overnight, she will become upset. She thinks that he is cheating on her and, worst of all, with his own wife.

Take the Offensive

You're the most important person in her life, so use your status to undermine their relationship. Because you're the wife, you can exploit her insecurities with little effort. Enhance the mistress's fear and self-doubt by planting clues that will show that your husband really prefers you.

1. When your husband is going to see her, ask him to bring back something for you. It could be anything from tampons to your favorite juice, but ask for a personal item. He may have to leave her early, before the store closes. You're annoying her because her lover is concerned about you when he's with her.

2. If the other woman discovers that your husband had a few hours to see her but didn't, that will start her doubting his love. Give him the chance to see her when you know he doesn't want to. If you know a special football game is on TV Saturday afternoon, plan to be away for those hours. If she finds out that he didn't try to visit her or even call her, she'll be annoyed.

3. Buy your husband a beeper. Are you smiling already? Beep him now and then; you'll be a nuisance to her.

4. Tell him that a strange woman is calling, muttering, "Sorry, wrong number," and hanging up. He may assume it's his girlfriend, and the next time he sees her he'll ask her if she's the caller. She'll start wondering who the second woman is.

5. Leave a note in his pocket signed with your love. A few pairs of undershorts with hearts or love symbols will annoy her, too. Plan it so he has only the fancy underwear clean when he's going to see her.

6. Go with him on the next business trip he takes. She'll never believe it's not a vacation, too.

7. Shop for a new mattress for your bed, even if you don't need one. If he tells her about your shopping, and he will because you're the topic of most of their conversations, she'll wonder what you're up to.

8. Before your husband leaves to visit her, embrace him and leave some telltale sign. The aroma of your cologne, a small hickey, or lipstick will annoy her. Stimulate him, if possible, and create the odors of sexual contact.

9. Give your husband a gift that he will wear all the time, such as a neck chain with a medal or charm. Let her stare at it. A watch inscribed "with love" on the back is also a good choice. The gift is a constant reminder of your affection for your husband and is symbolic of you.

10. Ask one of his relatives to throw you a birthday party or have some special-occasion dinner. You'll appear very entrenched in his life.

These are not unfair acts. After all, he is *your* husband and you have the right to hug and kiss him, travel with him, sign love notes to him, and carry on as a loving wife should.

6

FIGHTING BACK

Once you've decided that you want your marriage, analyze your strengths and weaknesses, explore your options, and develop your action plan. You'll examine strategies that should be used before he knows you've discovered his affair, others that should be used later, and some that should never be used except in the most dire of circumstances.

SEIZE THE INITIATIVE

Even if you let the relationship continue because you hope it will fizzle out, don't look the other way. If you ignore her, your husband will think you are a fool or don't want him. You should take action.

Recognize Your Power

You have a great deal of power over your husband, and even over the other woman. In fact, what you say and do is the primary ingredient in the success or failure of their affair. Yes, you can make them miserable together—so unhappy that they'll eventually prefer to be apart. They probably spend more time talking about you than doing anything else. You're definitely on their minds.

You're going to feel like giving him a swift kick in his posterior. At a minimum, you'll want to turn a cold shoulder to him. You certainly aren't going to feel like holding him tenderly in your arms or making love to him.

Once you get over the shock of his infidelity and get used to the hurt, you're going to be thinking about your reasons for avoiding him. At this point, you're probably saying to yourself, "Let him see what he's missing. Let him suffer." After all, your ego is on the line. You're waiting for him to beg on bended knee for your forgiveness.

These actions will save your ego but not your marriage. If you withdraw tenderness and sex, he'll have all the more reason to seek out his mistress. If you give him the silent treatment, he'll turn to her for conversation. Don't ostracize him unless you're willing to end your marriage.

This doesn't mean you should accept the affair or ignore your hurts and angers, but it does mean that you should view him as a jerk and a dummy rather than as the personification of evil.

If you still want him, you can take comfort in the fact that the odds are in your favor. You've heard that man is a creature of habit. Well, it's true, and you have habit on your side. He's familiar with you and comfortable with you and with the lifestyle he's leading. Dislocation and relocation aren't easy.

Will He Leave You?

Your husband's mistress may view herself as your replacement, and may feel that the affair is her audition for the role of wife. This perception is sometimes accurate, but in most cases, the husband views the other woman as merely a supplement.

A man sometimes seeks another woman because he finds you lacking in some attribute he considers important. The deficiencies that the man perceives can be numerous and varied. Often, they're neither reasonable nor realistic, but they're there.

A schoolteacher who's a camp counselor during the summer views that job as nothing more than a supplement to his regular job. He's not going to give up teaching to work in a summer camp. Similarly, your husband is not going to give you up to marry his mistress.

Are You Too Nasty or Selfish?

Some women drive their husbands away because they're too nasty. Could this be your situation? Look at the love behavior he learned when he was growing up, because it indicates the love behavior he's expecting now. If you're not as nice to him as his mother was, he may think you're too nasty.

If you're selfish, your husband is viewing your actions as infidelity. Look at your actions and see if they contribute to your mutual goals. You might need to refocus your thoughts.

Develop Your Action Plan

You might think of yourself as a straightforward, up-front person who says what's on her mind—not someone who plots, schemes, or manipulates. You may have to change your tactics. It's two against one.

Your husband is plotting and scheming so that he can have both you and his mistress or choose either one. His mistress is conniving to have him for herself, on her terms. You need to develop your own battle plan so that you can outmaneuver both of them.

Don't view your husband and his mistress as a unity that has your elimination as its sole purpose. In fact, their goals are quite different, and some of the techniques you will be learning will enable you to drive a wedge between them. These strategies are calculating, but they're hot and calculating.

Since the techniques that will work depend on the circumstances, a variety are described. They're presented in sequential order, so that if one doesn't work for you, you can readily move on to the next one. Use them when you know about the affair, but your husband isn't aware of your knowledge.

Evaluate Your Techniques

If he's had an affair before this one, you may feel you're following a familiar path in trying to end his extramarital relationship. Don't become complacent. A technique that worked before might not succeed now. He may have developed a resistance to it.

As a general rule, if he's a repeat offender, you'll need stronger techniques to break up his affair. If you use the same means, you'll need to apply them with greater intensity.

Indulge Yourself

Have you been devoting all your energies to your husband? Perhaps you've worked to put him through school, or you've helped him advance in his career while you've remained behind professionally. Or you've made sure your husband looked successful even if your wardrobe left much to be desired.

If you've been a devoted and self-sacrificing wife, you hurt even more deeply than other women when you discovered his infidelity. To make matters worse, you probably blamed yourself and became even more self-sacrificing. You said to yourself, "If only I were a better person," and you hoped and prayed he would recognize your goodness and forsake all others. You were nicer to him than ever, and did more for him, yet his adultery continued—even intensified.

You may discover that compared to you, the other woman is bitchy and dominating. She makes him feel that he's lucky to have her and is demanding of his time and attention. In that case, learn from her.

Strengthen Your Image

Your husband might have treated you as complacent and boring. He thinks he's superior to you, and feels that you've been treating him with deference because you thought he was superior. How could he misunderstand you so totally? Because he mistook niceness and kindness for weakness and subservience. Yes, you've been too thoughtful.

You may want him because of his strengths, but you may get to keep him because of his weaknesses. Stop being so nice. Point out his faults as well as his virtues. The more arrogant he is with you, the more faults you should remind him of.

Never let him think he is too good for you. When you use a comparison, and you tell him he's superior, make it clear he's superior to other men, not to you. Let him know he's brighter than Bill or neater than Ned. Never tell him that he's smarter than you are or has better reasoning powers than you do.

Dress Up

If you've been self-sacrificing, now is the time to stop. If he's better dressed than you are, improve your wardrobe. If his mistress is better dressed, get the clothes you'll need to compete for his attention. You may have thought of yourself as frugal, but he may have viewed you as frumpy. Change your image.

Brighten your color selection. Colors that women view as subtle, men view as washed out. By now, you should know your husband's color preferences. If you do, follow them in building your wardrobe. If you don't know his preferences, use blue, red, yellow, black, and white as your basic colors, and select outfits that have one or two of these colors. This is the time for facials, a new hair color, and other forms of self-improvement. You can win him back, or decide to dump him later. Either way, you'll be more appealing to other men. Indulge yourself if you've been too self-sacrificing.

DEALING WITH HIM

The following strategies will add to the discomfort he feels when he cheats on you. You need to stay on his mind constantly.

Securing His Workplace

Call him more at his office. Once a day is no longer enough. Call him at least three times a day for a brief hello. Make sure that one call is near lunchtime, one is just before he leaves work, and the other is at an unpredictable time. If he isn't in when you call, leave a message with his secretary or answering service, or on his answering machine. If he has a beeper, be sure to page him and ask him to call you back.

Give him a picture of you. The picture must be framed, so he has no excuse for not putting it on his desk or hanging it on the wall. Autograph the picture with a loving phrase such as, "To my darling husband." Make sure the picture is large enough for his co-workers to notice. In fact, let's hope the world notices it. Give him a second picture of you and the children with him. Maybe he'll take the hint.

It is better to be a nuisance for a short while than to concede victory to her. Make surprise visits to his office— stop by to see if he's free for lunch. When you're there, observe the way he interacts with his co-workers and you. Are you proudly introduced? Do you have a chance to talk freely to his co-workers? Do you feel that they know a lot about you and your family? Take the initiative and establish your own bonds with these people. Then it will be harder for him to leave you without sacrificing his job.

Need Him

If you want him, need him. Men often respond more strongly to need than they do to love. He may tell his mistress, "I can't leave my wife; she needs me." Believe it or not, he's expressing his real feelings.

You can use "need" to keep him, but you have to show the conditions and present them in the right manner, reflecting his uniqueness and individual self-worth. Here are three good ways of showing need:

1. I need you to help our son grow up to be a well-rounded man like you.
2. I need your help in remodeling the kitchen. You have impeccable taste.
3. I need you to make love to me. No one else can satisfy me the way you can.

Here are three ineffective ways of showing need, which don't make him feel needed for himself:

1. I need you to throw out the garbage.
2. I need your money.
3. I need you to buy juice at the market.

Become Unpredictable

Since your husband can see the other woman only on infrequent occasions, when he thinks he can sneak around without you finding out, he'll be planning each tryst or rendezvous with a great deal of care.

Your husband and the other woman are anticipating the moments they can share. A sudden cancellation of their plans can bring despair, especially to her, because he is a much larger part of her life than she is of his. Since you haven't let them know you're aware of the affair, they live in fear of being discovered. Use that fear to give them grief.

Change Plans

Here's a situation that illustrates how sudden changes in your plans can disrupt your husband's affair. Suppose you go out of town to visit your aunt during the third weekend in March. Think back to prior years. Your husband worked during the weekend before your trip so that he would have time free to see his mistress while you were away.

Now your trip is fast approaching. Your husband has arranged to work the coming Saturday in order to be free the following Saturday when you're away. Wait until Friday, then announce you'll be going a week early since he'll be busy at work. (That's right—put the onus on him.) It will be too late for him to change his work schedule and his mistress might have other plans anyway. You will have ruined their rendez-vous for next weekend without giving them a chance to get together this weekend.

Throw a Surprise Party

Most people enjoy surprise parties, but not a man who's having an affair. In fact, the surprise party can throw him into panic. He'll be concerned because you're able to pull something off and fool him. He depends on your predictabil-ity, and you've shown him that you're no longer predictable.

Also, with your friends and relatives around, he'll feel pressured into putting on a show of togetherness. Then your friends can tell him what a wonderful couple the two of you make.

If he's been trying to hide his affair, he might be using some of his friends to create alibis. He'll feel especially awkward about your conversations with them.

Use Sex

You wouldn't hesitate to use sex to save your marriage, would you? Your first thought is to withhold sex to punish your husband, but that will drive him into her arms. A better strategy is to intensify your sexual activity with him, espe-cially just before he sees her. His guilt over the affair should keep him from denying your sexual requests.

If he sees her on Wednesday evenings, when he is supposedly at a computer seminar, maximize his sexual performance on Tuesday night and again on Wednesday morning. By the time he sees her Wednesday evening, his ardor should have diminished substantially.

Use Food

You might not have thought of food as a weapon, but it can be part of your arsenal against the other woman. First, be sure you know your husband's favorite dishes and learn to cook them well. If you can't, get the recipes from his mother. Your husband will be comparing you with the other woman in the kitchen, as well as in the bedroom.

If you can, make sure he won't be seeing her directly from work and that he's well fed when he goes to see her. Encourage him to eat until he is stuffed. Then he'll be more likely to fall asleep once he gets there. With the right choice of ingredients, he'll start burping and farting. In any event, his sexual performance will be adversely affected as his body focuses its attention on digestion.

He won't reject your meals, especially if you cajole him into eating, for fear of arousing your suspicions. Tell him, "I know you've got that computer class tonight. I'm serving you a big meal so you won't get hungry during class."

This technique is especially useful if he's planning to have dinner with her. She's likely to be upset that he isn't looking forward to a meal with her. If you're lucky, she'll take it as a personal rejection.

Use Money

Just as you can use sex and food to fight your husband, you can also use money. The key is to make sure he has less to spend on her. She may think that his financial position is deteriorating. Even worse, she may think he's losing interest in her.

It's easy to control the purse strings if he turns over his paycheck to you. Otherwise, just make sure you increase the household expenditures and spend more on yourself so less is left for her.

Use Pranks

If you've been taught from your earliest childhood that fighting fair is morally righteous, but that tricks are unsavory, then view these techniques merely as pranks.

Confront Them Indirectly

Once you discover that your husband is having an affair, and you know who the other woman is, you'll feel that you must confront them. It will be almost impossible for you to resist that urge, but don't face them yet. You can always do so later, at a time and place *you* choose. Keep your self-control, so you can manipulate the situation. Treat the information you've gained as an asset. Use it rather than reveal it.

If you know about their affair, but they don't know that they've been discovered, you're in a position of power over them. Knowledge doesn't always give you power, but it certainly does here. Now that you've discovered their relationship, you can create havoc within it. Try these techniques first.

Hint at the Affair

Hint at your husband's affair before you confront him directly. This is your opportunity to make the nasty statements about his mistress that you didn't mention earlier.

Here's how to start the conversation with your husband: "Would you believe the nerve of that woman? I got into quite a heated argument at the store. While I was waiting in line at the checkout counter, a woman who works with me told me that you're having an affair with Sandy." (Mention the name of his mistress.) "Well, I told her that you're loving and loyal and faithful." (Build him up, then get your claws ready.) "Then I told her that even if you were unfaithful, you'd have much better taste than to go anywhere near something like Sandy. I let her know you wouldn't have anything to do with a low-class, stuck-up, sleazy whore like her." (I bet you're enjoying this part.)

Give him the opportunity to deny his relationship with Sandy. Don't challenge him or disagree if he says he's not having an affair with her. (You could be wrong, and if you're not, you'll have many opportunities to confront him later.) Give him the chance to echo the negative things you've said about her. If he's having an affair, let him talk himself out of it. If he makes negative statements about her, but continues the affair, you'll be gaining information from his statements. If he says good things about her, then you're really in trouble because he's enjoying her beyond the sex. You'll need to use the stronger strategies.

If you're willing to fight fire with fire—or with water, depending on what's necessary—these are additional strategies for you.

Use the Two-Boyfriend Gambit

Now that you've had your chance to say these nasty things about his mistress, you'll be able to do even more damage if you still don't let on that you've discovered the affair.

Here's your chance to expand on the theme that she's a slut, only worse. Tell your husband that the woman you've been describing has two lovers and that they don't know about each other. Then give a general description of one lover which could apply to a number of men, including your husband, and another lover who seems more appealing. If you want to dig your nails deeper into his psyche, tell him that you heard that she's really in love with the second man.

MANIPULATING YOUR HUSBAND

Now that you know about his mistress, and he knows you know, you'll feel like telling your husband that she's dumb, uncultured, uncaring, and a general all-around lowlife. Resist that temptation. If you say negative things about her, he'll leap to her defense. You don't want him thinking about her good qualities, do you?

Praise Her

How can you get your husband to think negative thoughts about his mistress? There is an effective technique, but you'll find it quite unpleasant. You'll have to praise her, but when you do so by means of comparison, never compare her with yourself. Hold her up to other women you and your husband know, and never put yourself down.

If she's sexy, but not as much as your neighbor Suzy, tell him that she's sexier than Suzy. When he reflects on what you said, he'll bring to mind her imperfections and start thinking about the fact that she's not as sexy as Suzy.

If she's relatively smart, tell him that she's very bright, and that you can't think of any gaps in her intellect. You'll be prompting him to look for these gaps.

The idea is to induce him to think negative thoughts about her. Just as your criticism of her could evoke his praise, your admiration might evoke his criticism.

Make Him Feel Inferior

When you're praising the other woman, you can use an alternate technique at the same time to convince your husband that his mistress will never stay with him over the long run. If all else fails, compare him to the other woman. Of course, there should be an element of truth in what you say, so emphasize the areas where she's superior. Tell him you understand why he wants her. After all, she's more educated and attractive than he is, and comes from a better family. She probably earns more money. When he's with her, he will think about what you said and start looking at her as a competitor.

The idea is to make him feel inferior, so that he'll believe he could never maintain her interest. Here are some of the statements you could make:

1. "She's a lot brighter than you are."
2. "You don't have the breeding to travel in her social circle."
3. "At some point she'll get tired of having a sugar daddy and want a real relationship instead."
4. "You look older than her father."
5. "She's too ambitious to hang around with a man in your income bracket."

Push Him Toward Her

Doesn't it sometimes seem that the wife does all the work and the mistress has all the fun? You're cooking and cleaning while she's wining and dining. If they were together day in and day out, the glamour would wear thin rather quickly.

Why not push him toward her? Give them a chance to be together without the excitement and glamour. Without makeup, hair in curlers, and in a bathrobe, she probably looks no more exciting than you do.

Team Up with Her

Most of these strategies are designed to drive a wedge between your husband and his mistress. Here's a different approach—one that's designed to lull him into a false sense of security and then put him on the defensive.

This isn't easy, but it's effective. You've got to bite your tongue while you're swallowing your pride. It is a last-straw technique, but you might want to use it: Develop a rapport with his mistress, go shopping with her, have lunch with her, become friendly.

At first your husband will be delighted that his wife and mistress get along so well. He'll think he has the best of both worlds—that the three of you are one happy family. Let him fantasize for a while, and build up his hopes and dreams of keeping both of you.

Once he's comfortable, turn on him. Tell him that the two of you decided that if you are going to share a man, you're going to find a better man than he is. Tell him that the two of you are going to take a long trip together without him. Let him worry that he'll lose both of you. Of course, he will tell her what you said. She may confirm it, but even if she denies it, he will think she is lying. He will panic and seek safety by mending his life with you. Then, you can double-cross her and reestablish your bond with him.

Emphasize Your Compatibility

At this stage, he's focusing on the pleasures that come from being with her and the burdens that come from staying with you. What an unfair comparison! Now's the time to remind him why you and he are so compatible, and point out why he'll never be fully comfortable with her.

If she's much younger, point out how you and he have been shaped by the historical events of your youth. Show him that they really amounted to shared experiences, even before you met. Let him know that she doesn't have the same frame of reference, so that he's going to have to give her a history lesson whenever he makes reference to some event in the past.

Discuss the fun you shared together, and the progress you have made toward your goals. Let him know that if he changes wives, his boss and co-workers will view him as rearranging his priorities. Focus on the values you share with him. Now is the time to bring up religion, family, country, and other things he holds dear. Emphasize the values that she doesn't share, and point out their importance to him over a lifetime.

Appeal to His Loyalty

Let him know the harm that his affair is causing you and the children. Be specific about how he is hurting the family. If the children were taunted in school, be sure to repeat these comments to him.

He might not be prepared to end his affair. Instead, he might rationalize his actions or tell you that you're overreacting. Be prepared with your reply.

Appeal to His Self-Interest

You might think your husband would give up his affair once he realizes how much harm he's causing you and the children. However, if he persists in the relationship, the next step is to show him how much harm he's doing to himself. At this point, he loves himself more than he loves you, so an appeal to his self-interest is more likely to succeed.

Let him know that the breakup will damage his prestige, reputation, and social standing in the community. Be specific. For instance, tell him that one of his favorite clubs doesn't let divorced members remain. Let him know that a number of people will think he's a scatterbrain, a philanderer, or worse.

Also let him know that the divorce will cost him power and money. Then drop a hint about the expensive car you're now looking at, or the tuition you'll be needing when you enroll for your further education.

EVALUATING YOUR COMPETITION

When you discover the mistress, you're going to feel more than hurt and anger. After the initial shock and sadness, you'll start comparing her attributes with yours. You're wondering what your husband sees in her when he has you. Perhaps you're saying to yourself, "She's younger but I'm more sophisticated," or "She's classier, but I'm more fun."

At some point, you'll be making an overall assessment of her positives and negatives compared with yours. You might not be doing so consciously and deliberately, but it's hard to avoid. Besides, you're better off knowing your competition. Then you can design a more effective battle plan if you want to fight to keep your husband.

You've heard that opposites attract, yet you've also heard that birds of a feather stick together. Both of these expressions point you partially in the direction of the strategy you should follow.

By now, you should know your husband's concept of his perfect mate, and how you differ from this ideal. As painful as it may be, make the same comparison between his fantasy and the other woman. Then, somewhat gleefully, you'll see how she differs from his ideal.

You'll probably find that she's no closer to being his ideal mate than you are. In fact, you're much closer to what he really wants. Go ahead and say what you're thinking: "I don't know what he sees in her." If she's clearly not his ideal woman, why is he bothering with her? The answer is that she has the opposite attributes that he's looking for. If your husband's idea of perfection is a woman who is good-looking and a superb cook, and you're attractive but lousy in the kitchen, the other woman might be homely but a good cook. Then your solution is simple if you want your husband— improve your cooking skills.

The other woman might have the opposite attributes from yours, based on your husband's concept of his ideal mate, but she lacks many of the positive qualities you do have. If this is your situation, don't despair. There's very little chance he'll leave you for her. You'll be able to use your positive features, and her lack of them, to draw him closer to you.

On the other hand, you might discover that she has the same attributes you do, but more of them. Let's suppose that your husband's ideal mate is bright, sexy, rich, well-educated, and cultured, and that you have these attributes to some degree. If she's smarter, sexier, has more money, and had finer schooling and a more cultured background than you, you have every reason to worry.

If you focus more on her similarities to you than on her differences, she's a greater threat. After all, your husband did choose you above all others, at least at one time, so there must be a lot about you that he does like. If he sees the same good points in her, you're facing real competition for his emotions and affections.

What You Need to Know About Her

Have you heard the expression, "Know Your Enemy"? It certainly applies here. The more you know about his mistress, the better able you'll be to fight back.

The more information you have about this woman, the better it will be for you. Reliable information is hard to find, but here are ten facts you should uncover if you can:

1. Discover her religious beliefs. You'll be able to use this information to increase her feelings of guilt.

2. Discover her superstitions. You'll be able to use them to increase her fears and anxieties.

3. Find out when she was born. Then you'll be able to keep him away from her on her birthday, and you'll be able to emphasize her age or immaturity, as the case may be.

4. Find out about her intellectual ability (or lack of it) and her educational successes and failures. Whether you discover that she's too superior to bother with your husband or too inferior to ever catch him, you'll be able to put this information to use.

5. You can put her medical history to use, too. Perhaps she has a tendency to ulcers.

6. Find out who her enemies are. You might be able to enlist their help in your quest for your mate or use them as scapegoats if your plans backfire.

7. Discover her recreational activities and hobbies and compare them with your husband's. You might have to show up at the tennis court after all.

8. Her personal and family history will also give you clues as to the ways in which you can compete against her. Perhaps you'll discover numerous broken marriages, strings of affairs, illegitimate children, and other skeletons in the closet.

9. Find out what you can about her employer and her job. Her boss or her clients might be vulnerable to your pressure.

10. Find out about her financial resources. Your strategy will differ depending on whether your husband is supporting her or she's funding the affair.

Her Birthday

Once you've discovered her birthday, you can put that information to good use in disrupting their relationship. A mistress's birthday is an extremely important event to her. She recognizes that her lover (your husband) can't spend holidays with her. After all, they're family events, and he has to be with you. However, her birthday is a different matter. He'll make an extra effort to spend it with her.

You never thought you would care about your husband's mistress's birthday, but you should. This is the day you want to make absolutely certain your husband spends with you. Don't even let him near the phone if you can exert that much control.

She'll be waiting eagerly for his phone call, and the fact that he doesn't call will cause a rift between them. She won't believe his story that he couldn't get free for a minute to call.

Fidelity to the Mistress

A mistress views herself as occupying a special and unique role in the man's life, seeing herself as his soul mate and confidante in a way that his wife could never be. Also, in her own way, she demands fidelity. She might be able to accept the time and attention that he devotes to you, since you were there first. Acceptance of you is part of the bargain she struck with herself when she agreed to become his mistress. She is even resigned to his continuing sexual involvement with you.

The one thing a mistress won't accept is his involvement with another woman. To accept such a compromise means that she is less than a mistress, and in fact is just one of many casual sex partners. Since a key to the husband-mistress relationship is true openness of communication, his secret relationship with any other woman would be devastating.

Also, you could tell his present mistress about his prior affairs, so she won't feel unique and special.

In fact, there even are situations in which a wife can't enforce fidelity and will let the husband have a mistress, knowing that the woman will enforce the fidelity rule against others. It's ironic, isn't it, to think of the mistress demanding and enforcing fidelity, but it's an important part of the mistress system.

One wife used a past mistress, who gave up the affair for the sake of the children, to get rid of her husband's current mistress. When the first mistress heard about the second one, there were fireworks, and the husband went back to the wife.

The "Two-Mistress" Gambit

A fast way to get rid of his mistress is to convince her that he's cheating on *her*, that she isn't the true love of his life. You can do so, even if you've never met, if you plant the right clues.

The thought might have crossed her mind that since he's cheating on you, he would also cheat on her. But this idea never occurs to some mistresses—at least, not without prompting. There might not be another woman (in addition to you and the mistress), but you want her to think there is.

Think of the obvious clues to infidelity and plant them. Put lipstick (not your color) on his shirt. Or put a blond hair on his suit (assuming neither you nor the mistress is blond). Better yet, put a love note (not in your handwriting) in his jacket pocket.

Once you know who the other woman is, then you know which of your female acquaintances you can trust. After all, you'll need an accomplice in supplying the blond hair and the love note. If your friend is even bolder, she can call your husband at the mistress's apartment. When he's taking the kids to see their grandparents, you'll have the mistress believing that he's with another woman.

ENLIST HELP

You might feel that you can't fight his mistress by yourself. Fortunately, you don't have to. There are many sources of help, including your family, his family (hopefully), friends, and the clergy.

Your Adult Children

Adultery and its aftermath will affect your children, but it gives you greater leverage if they are grown. Tell your grown children the truth. The closer your daughter is to her father, the more she can help you. She'll tell him all the things you feel and can't say, and express her disappointment in him.

What about your son? Many women expect that sons will take the father's side. They think there is a camaraderie of spirit of "Boys will be boys," and "He'll understand." Your son might feel this way if he is going through puberty. In most cases, he cares about you and your pain of infidelity, and will be on your side, too.

Your Parents

Don't hide the affair from your parents. They are likely to be on your side and will provide moral support and good advice. But can they convince him to stop? Maybe they can talk about the grandchildren and how they're affected without the anger you might show. It's worth a try.

What about *his* parents? They might be on his side unless they're concerned about the grandchildren. Grandparents become worried when they feel the grandchildren don't love them as much as before, will forget them, or start disliking them because Grandma and Grandpa aren't angry at Dad.

Your extended family can also be an important source of emotional support in your struggle. First, you've got to know which of your relatives he genuinely likes. Hopefully, your communication with your husband has been sufficiently open for him to express his true feelings about the various members of your family. Organize gatherings, inviting over the family members whose company he enjoys. Seeing your relatives and feeling that special camaraderie with them will make him think about how much he'll miss them. No matter how interesting his mistress is, it would be very difficult for her to match all the fun your relatives collectively provide.

His family can also help save your marriage. The question is, will they? Even if you can't count on their deliberate help, you can use them to influence your husband's behavior. Extend an invitation to them to join you for a weekend or the holidays. His family will sense the tensions in your household that arise when he's out with the other woman. Because your husband would try to make his family feel a certain solidarity, comfort, and a reliving of the good old days, he'll be on his best behavior and stay home more. That should make the mistress even more uncertain about him and more demanding. Hopefully, she'll show enough negative traits that his desires for her will diminish.

When you tell his family about his affair, do so one at a time, and not at the family dinner. If you ruin their meal talking about the affair, especially if it's supposed to be a festive occasion, the family could get quite upset with you for your insensitivity. Informing them one at a time gives you an opportunity to see who is the most shocked, who is the most supportive of you, who seems happy, who offers to help, and who you feel you can trust. Also, if you gather his family to discuss your husband's wanderings, they might react as a group and support him regardless of his actions. Divide and conquer.

The Clergy

The clergy can help save your marriage, but only if they know about your problems. Tell them early, when you find out, to increase their opportunities to help. At a minimum, they'll revive and reemphasize his feelings of guilt. Hopefully, they'll also spark fond memories and his feelings of affection for you.

Her Husband

If she's married, perhaps you should tell her husband about the affair and ask for his help in ending it. Or do you want to teach your husband and his mistress a lesson by having an affair with her husband?

Having an affair with her husband won't bring about the revenge you seek. Its most likely effect is that your husband and his mistress will feel less pressure to end their own arrangement. They might even feel that your later actions justified their early ones.

Before you embark upon either of these paths, you ought to discover certain things about the mistress's husband and his relationship with her. Most important, you want to know whether he's faithful to her or is having an affair with someone else. (This gets complicated, doesn't it?)

If he's a good husband and doesn't deserve his wife cheating on him, let your husband know it's a sure bet she has other lovers.

STRATEGIES YOU SHOULD AVOID

Using the Children as a Weapon

Picture this scenario: You're sitting at the dinner table with your children. Your husband is with his mistress. Then, your oldest asks, "Where's Daddy?" and you tearfully answer, "Daddy is with his girlfriend."

If you followed this scenario through to its conclusion, you'd picture your children telling your husband that he's not supposed to have a girlfriend, and that they need him and love him and don't want him to go away. At first glance, it seems that they'll be a powerful weapon in your battle.

This is a strong weapon, and one that shouldn't be used. For one thing, you would be causing your children extreme anguish and distress. For another, your husband would feel that someone who uses children as a weapon is unloving. He could resolve to leave you and fight for custody of them.

Bribes

You might be tempted to pay your husband's mistress to stay away from him. Resist this temptation, for you might lose your money as well as your husband. It's highly unlikely that you can get her to leave town, and if she doesn't, it might still be difficult to keep her and your husband apart.

If you insist on bribing her to stay away from your husband, at least have the good sense not to pay the bribe in one lump sum. Send her weekly amounts while she remains away.

You might be able to bribe her indirectly—especially if she is naive or impoverished. Arrange for her to win a cruise at a time your husband must be home for business. The longer the cruise the better. Get the least expensive accommodations and make sure the cruise ticket is · non-transferable and one-way. The time apart is likely to make them unbond, especially if it's difficult to reach each other by phone. Even better, she may meet someone else and lose interest in him.

Threats

You've probably thought up numerous threats you'd like to direct against your husband or his mistress. Unfortunately, most of these won't work in your favor.

First, some threats are illegal, even if you don't carry out the act you've threatened. Intimidating her with violence will get you in trouble. His mistress would like nothing better than to have you put away in a jail or mental institution.

Second, don't threaten your husband with physical harm. He could do worse to you.

Third, if you're going to threaten anyone, threaten her. Tell her that you'll damage her reputation in church or in the neighborhood. Call her "home wrecker," "bitch," or "walking sleaze," but stay away from criticizing her professional skills. She could sue you! Also, be cautious about trying to have her fired from her job—your husband might then decide to support her.

Murder—The Ultimate Revenge

Your hurt and anger over his infidelity might have no limits. At times you're so furious that you want to kill him. Perhaps you daydream of ways to get rid of him permanently. But before you actually plot his demise, you need to deal with a number of practical issues.

First, you would be violating your own conscience. If he's the father of your children, you would be plagued by overwhelming guilt. You would also be suspect number one.

Second, it's highly likely that you would be caught. The police look for motive and opportunity, and as the wife of a philanderer, you would certainly qualify.

Third, you might fail in your attempt and get killed or injured in the process. What if he's severely hurt by the gunshot, knife, poison, fall, or attempted drowning, but isn't killed? He might need many years of painstaking care, and you might feel sufficiently guilty that you would provide it.

And fourth: your children would never forgive you.

Snare His Affection for Her

If your relationship has reached the stage where he'll talk about the affair, you might be able to reestablish yourself as his confidante. This isn't going to be fun, but it *is* highly effective. Tell him that you don't want to be shut out of his life completely. Then go further and tell him that you want to vicariously share the joy he feels in loving her. Encourage him to bring forth all the warmth and affection he feels for her. Be very careful not to puke while you're listening.

THE IMPASSE

Perhaps you and your mate have reached the point that little is left of your relationship. You share a home, but you know his heart is elsewhere. In short, he's seeing someone else openly. You're ignored as a lover, and it's just a matter of time before you and he formally bury the relationship by parting ways completely. Still, you hope to rekindle his love and his interest in you. Here are steps that can help your cause if you carry them through. It's difficult, because you have to control yourself, but it usually pays off.

REDEFINE YOUR RELATIONSHIP

Change the Ambiance

Change the ambiance of your house to an upbeat, positive, and fun mood. Even if you can't manage to exude joy, at least once a week invite friends over who like to have fun. Party, play cards, listen to music, or rent a movie and make pop-corn. When your husband has a boring time out, he'll think it would have been better to stay home.

Start Projects

Begin projects around the house that you know would arouse his curiosity and that he would enjoy doing. It could be building a magazine rack, doing a gigantic puzzle, organizing a Tuesday night bridge game, taking up gourmet cooking, or redecorating the hallway.

Create a Social Whirl

Begin a life for yourself outside the house. You won't enjoy everything you do if you're in this hiatus, but don't appear defeated. You enjoyed many things in the past without him, so dwell on those activities. Put a smile on your face, or you'll look undesirable even to those you once rejected.

Lift Yourself Up

Get into a self-improvement mood. Take up jogging or buy a new wardrobe; take a step forward. Attend a class or join a group that will provide new things. A few new ideas can change your outlook.

Become Roommates

Declare your relationship to be that of "roommates." Treat him as a roommate and show all the courtesies and mind-your-own-business attitudes you would to a houseguest.

If your presence makes him feel guilty and unhappy, and your home is an emotional funeral parlor, obviously he's going to scram as soon as he can financially do so. However, if staying there with you is emotionally equal to having moved out because you're a pleasant, nonsexual companion, he would just as soon stay put. It's less hassle than moving and cheaper.

It's important to have him nearby. Otherwise, you can't influence him very much. Of course, let him know that you feel detached from him and free to do whatever you wish.

Use Sexual Discretion

If you and your husband are just roommates, don't flaunt a sexual relationship in front of him. In fact, agree not to bring dates home for sex when the other person is there. Reason with him that it would be awkward for the new sexual partners as well as for each other. At the very least, try to implement this policy for a few months. If he were to see you

with another in a situation he knows is sexual, any posses-
sive feeling could be lost and he'll make even further
attempts to forget you.

Above all, try to look as serene as you can when you are
with him. Happiness makes a person attractive, irresistible,
and most appealing.

The Ultimatum

"Give her up or else!" This is your trump card, but it's also
your last resort. If it doesn't succeed, you either have to back
down or proceed with the action you've threatened (usually
divorce).

In this case, inaction is equivalent to backing down. If you
let him continue living under the same roof with you, you're
then giving tacit approval to his affair. That's why you should
leave the ultimatum for last.

Kick Him Out

If you've really decided to end the marriage, you're usually
better off if you kick him out. Don't remain under the same
roof with him and don't give him possession of the house.
There's an old adage that possession is nine-tenths of the
law. Well, proprietorship isn't that important, but it does
count. Your husband will probably leave with only some
prodding on your part since he recognizes that he's at fault.

He could really miss you and want you back, but don't wait on it.

If You Ever Leave

If you still want him, and you're willing to risk the house, move out. She's expecting to move in once you leave, but he might have other plans. He might value his privacy, he might be concerned that you'll move back, or he might decide he could have many women. If she's not invited to move in, or this invitation doesn't come promptly, she could become angry enough to end the affair.

7

MANIPULATING HIS MISTRESS

When you have reached the stage at which his affair is out in the open, you'll need to meet his mistress without confronting her. This strategy can be used to win back his love.

Of course, you can decide at any point that your husband is a rat and heel and isn't worth the bother. If so, you can stop trying to win him back. What is important is that *you* have the choice, so you don't lose by default.

MEET HER

Make it a point to meet his mistress, if you can. Remember: You're not doing this for the purpose of scratching her eyes out or causing other physical damage, but so that you can start manipulating her.

There are many ways you can meet her. Just call her up and suggest it. She may ask who you are and why you want to meet her, so be prepared to say that you have something—a friend, for example—in common. Give her your name: she'll be curious to meet you. Create an excuse—tell her that she has been recommended to participate in a survey and can choose lunch at a restaurant of her choice. Suggest a meeting in neutral territory, neither in your place nor hers. You may have the opportunity to meet at your home or her apartment at a later date, but that encounter can wait.

Don't meet her with your husband present. He'll feel he has to choose between the two of you, and you don't want him to make the choice until you've shifted the odds in your favor.

It's going to be very hard not to say what you really think. You'll get callouses from biting your tongue, but don't let on that you've discovered her. Even if you mention that your husband is having an affair, don't indicate that you know he is having an affair with her.

MENTION THE OTHER MISTRESS

Now you have a second opportunity to use the two mistresses gambit. If she's thirty-five with red hair, tell her about your husband's twenty-five-year-old blonde. Since you know when he was seeing his mistress and when he spent his time elsewhere, ascribe these other time periods to his younger mistress.

Now you can make a few of the snide remarks that you've been saving up. Tell her that, in addition to the flaxen beauty he cares about, your husband is "fooling around with an empty-headed woman in her midthirties," according to the grapevine. You can describe her in pejorative terms and diminish their relationship.

Be careful that you don't let her know that you are on to her, or go overboard in your condemnation of her. You want her to feel that she was clever enough to discover her secret problems, not that she was found out and told off. You want her hostility to be directed to your husband, not to you.

If your excuses to meet with her fail, then tell the truth. Tell her that you're his wife and that you and she have much at stake. Ask to meet for a brief chat.

PRETEND CONSENT

If you can discover a great deal about your husband's mistress, there's an additional strategy you can use once you meet her. The purpose of this maneuver is to convince her that you support him in having an affair, and that he has no intention of leaving you. Of course, you're being deceitful, but restoring your marriage may be more important than a good-conduct medal.

When you meet her, repeat back to her some of the things you've discovered. If you can, make reference to her family, school, and job. Then say "Harry (your husband) has told me so much about you." You've discovered this information from other sources, but you can convince her that you found it out from Harry. She'll believe that he really does confide in you.

This revelation will stir many nasty thoughts within her. She'll feel that she isn't really his confidante and soul mate because he's confiding in you. You'll be compounding these feelings if you let her know you wanted him to have an affair, and that you've helped him choose the woman. You can say "Karen, you've been carefully chosen." Since these statements are totally at odds with your true feelings, practice them a few times first. She'll start believing that he won't do anything without your consent, let alone have an affair behind your back, so that she has no chance of getting him away from you.

TALK ABOUT YOUR HUSBAND'S MIDLIFE CRISIS

If the mistress hasn't given up by now, tell her about your husband's midlife crisis. Here the goal is to raise questions about your husband's health and to subtly denigrate the quality of his affections for her.

Begin with a statement such as, "I want to thank you for helping Harry through his midlife crisis." What you really mean is, "You're giving me a midlife crisis." This is not, however, the time for truthfulness.

You can point out that many men his age (whatever that age is) take up dangerous activities. Tell her that you wouldn't want your husband to die while mountain climbing or car racing, and that if he's going to die when he's away from you, you would rather it happen in another woman's arms. At the very least, she'll start worrying that he will drop dead while they are having sex. It's hard to think of a greater damper on their ardor.

Then diminish her relationship with him by telling her that for years you've been encouraging him to get a "hobby," that like other men he needs his "playthings," and that you understand his fooling around. These pejorative words will lower her status, but not to the point that they should lead to a physical confrontation.

BEFORE YOU GIVE UP

If your husband has told you that he wants to divorce you and marry her, you might be hurt, even despondent, but don't give up. Here's an effective strategy, but only if you're willing to start your life over. This is not usually suitable for a woman with children, but consider the plan anyway.

Tell her that she's won, and you're willing to concede defeat graciously. (Of course, you're lying, but don't let that stop you.) Now is the time to invite her to your home. Tell her that you want to make her adjustment easier. (That's another lie.)

Show her the bedroom, and reinforce what she might already know—that her husband-to-be snores, hogs the covers, farts at night, and is always asking for snacks that are prepared in a special way. Then show her how he likes his clothes folded, his shirts laundered, and his pants pressed.

She'll also need to know about your husband's vitamins and medications, and don't forget the dire consequences if he misses one of these little pills. If she wants a peaceful existence with him, tell her that she should never move any of his papers, touch his dresser or night table, or throw out any of his old clothes or newspapers. He keeps *everything*, including broken down old radios, cars, coffee makers, and TV sets for parts.

Give her the chance to run away.

8

SAVING YOUR MARRIAGE

Your husband may have cheated, but you *can* preserve and renew your marriage. To do so, surround yourself with supportive friends. Then, examine your ideas of marriage and discard the myths that hurt you to recapture fidelity.

DO YOU STILL WANT HIM?

These indicators can help you decide your potential for happiness with him:

1. Is he there for you whenever you really need him?
2. Does he talk freely to you—almost as if he were talking out loud to himself?

3. Is he friendly and affectionate with your family and friends?
4. Does he introduce you with pride to people you meet when you're together?
5. Does he frequently seek your companionship?
6. When something unexpected happens in his life, does he call you right away?
7. If he's upset or overjoyed, does he share these feelings with you first?
8. Is he exclusively dependent on you for the enjoyment of fun activities together?
9. Does he consult you for your ideas whenever he does something that has long-term consequences? (i.e., would he buy a car without asking your opinion?)
10. When he talks about the future, are you always in the picture?

If the answers to the above questions are "yes," you're foremost in his heart and mind.

EVALUATE YOUR DISPARITY INDEX

You and your husband have differences in attitudes that keep you interesting to each other. The disparity between you and him must be comfortable and rewarding, not shocking and unacceptable. Interests change over time, affecting both your disparity indexes. Too much of it will cause you excitement instead of pleasure.

The media portrays a great amount of diversity because it's entertaining, "playing" opposites against each other, such as a conservative man and a liberal woman, or a city girl and a country boy. In the media, disparity is resolved, but not in reality.

Part of loving is giving into the other person's whims, but make sure that giving in doesn't interfere with things that really matter. If each of you wins once in a while, there's a happy balance.

If the disparity increases, with changes that you won't tolerate, the mutual rifts begin. Lifestyle changes will trouble you the most.

There are five clues that can indicate major changes ahead:

1. New political views.
2. Increase or decrease of sexual desire.
3. Family changes.
4. Changes in perception of longevity.
5. New moral values.

He's changed, but have you? He may think that your attitudes, which he once considered cute, are now oppressive. Fussing about things that never bothered him before means trouble. Monitor your disparity to achieve compatibility.

INCREASE YOUR HAPPINESS QUOTIENT

There are risks to trusting your mate again. You may be concerned that he would view forgiveness as a weakness, that he is more likely to have another affair and that you would forgive him again. There are no sure answers to your concerns, but you can increase your probability for success by knowing him even better.

How well do you know your husband? If you really know him, you could answer these ten basic questions:

1. What's the most fun he's ever had?
2. How much money would he need to be happy?
3. What was his favorite vacation?
4. What's his favorite movie? Television show? Game? Hobby?
5. When would he like to retire? What would he do?
6. How does he want to be remembered?
7. How would he change society if he could?
8. He has three wishes—what would he wish for?
9. What gift would he consider most memorable?
10. How would he like to celebrate his next birthday?

If you don't know the answers to all these questions, then ask him. A positive statement, then a question, may be your best way of getting information if he's resistant. Use the ideas in a statement to see if you're right, such as, "Wasn't our best vacation in Florida?"

INCREASE YOUR COMPATIBILITY

Basic Needs

If he's at ease, it's comfortable for him to live with you. A mutually acceptable comfort zone makes it easy for you to live with him. Listen to his complaints and express yours. You'll understand each other's less apparent but important needs.

Quiet Time

Observe how much quiet time your husband needs to think, to accomplish his mental tasks, and to recover from the exhaustion of the day. If you talk too much by his standards, he'll avoid you. If you are too quiet, he'll turn on the television.

If your mate has too much "down" time, he'll get restless. Increase the length of your conversations or let music set the mood. A day at a stadium or at a noisy festival can make him long for the peace of home. If he has little quiet time, minimize distracting noise. Talk less when he is tired.

Favorite Foods

Scintillate his taste buds with favorite foods. Cooking *your* favorite meal doesn't please him as much as *his* favorite meal. Cook something he really likes on the weekend. If a chili dog is his favorite, serve the best chili dog in town.

The Comfort at Home

If your husband is a big man, he needs big items. Little chairs, little towels probably annoy him. Buy the household goods you like, but keep your big guy in mind.

You and your spouse have different standards for neatness. If he's surrounded by a mess, he won't be happy with you. If you expect everything to be perfect, that's too demanding on him. He needs the freedom to put a glass on a tabletop, or use the guest towel, or leave his magazines around. If you're opposites, at least set aside areas of the house where you each can do as you please.

New Ideas

New ideas can strengthen your relationship. You don't need great ideas, only new ones. You wouldn't think of wearing the same dress every day or serving the identical meal for lunch and dinner, so don't use the same ideas every day. New topics of conversation shows you're mentally alert.

His Conscience

Know your mate's conscience, so you don't create serious moral conflicts except for his adultery. Your guidelines should be how much he identifies with the values of his family, his church, and his culture.

YOUR FRIENDSHIPS HELP

Cross-bonding

When bonds of friendship occur between opposite sexes, you have a friend who can speak to your husband man to man. You can return the favor by being an ally who can have a woman-to-woman chat with his wife.

It's not likely that you and your husband will enjoy every couple as a twosome. Perhaps you like one spouse and just barely tolerate the other. Nevertheless, as a couple they are dedicated to each other and their closeness supports your ideals. Cross-bond with such couples, and become friendly with the likable half.

The cross-bonding increases pressure against adultery. Your men friends who care about their wives don't mind standing up for their values and will not applaud adulterous encounters. These pals can recognize potential problems before you can because they know how your husband acts with women when you're not with him. It's comforting to have a buddy watching out for your interests.

If your husband continues to cheat, tell his close friends. This should be the final step. If they are your friends, too, they'll encourage him to give up the other woman.

Your friends are one of your best defenses against adultery. If you are bonding with happy couples, they'll keep tabs on your husband. They may not tell you they saw your husband with another woman, but they will tell him they saw him with someone else and defend you.

Know His Friends

Your husband's buddies might want to be part of a male-only group, perhaps because they are interested in womanizing. If your husband is out with the boys, check to see that they really are doing what he told you they were doing. Welcome them at your place. It helps you size them up.

Some men don't confide in women especially when it comes to their buddies. Confiding in his friends may mean he's not confiding in you. Meet these buddies and start networking with one of their wives who can introduce you to the others. They are probably eager to meet you and want to figure out what their husbands are up to.

Your husband's friends influence him more than you suspect, and may be as important to him as you are. You can have a major impact on his life and his relationship with you if you are friends with his friends. But do you really know them? At a minimum, you could say that you know his friends if you can answer the following ten questions:

1. What are their real names?
2. What are their addresses?
3. What are their telephone numbers?
4. What are their spouses' names?
5. What are their occupations?
6. How did they meet your husband?

7. How long have they been friends?
8. How often do they get together?
9. What are the highlights of the friendship?
10. When are they antagonists?

Each friend affects your husband. You can predict your husband's state of mind by what friend he's focusing on at the moment. If your husband is hassled and would like quiet, he'll talk about Frank, his fishing buddy. If your husband is bored, he'll talk about Bob's wild parties.

Know His Co-Workers

If work is the only place where the lovers can see each other, cheating takes away from your husband's time at the job. Your husband's co-workers will probably discourage his affairs at work since they will have to cover up for him by doing his share. Your husband's employer may fear that his cheating at work will lead to a lawsuit on sexual harassment. In fact, the company could be implicated if it knew of the affair.

Visit your husband's workplace without being a pest. You can, if you learn about his work environment and are friendly to his companions. The more they like you, the more they will look out for your interests.

It's easy to check on your husband if you work together. Even if you're not employed by the same company, you can commute together, meet for lunch, go to each other's work events and office parties. His job is much more than his employment. It involves people, and you should meet and ask about them. Otherwise, your husband's co-workers may think you don't care about him. That makes women more aggressive in seeking his companionship.

Enhance Family Values

If you can reinstill family values, renewing his adultery will be more difficult. These are ten events where the family gathers and reinforces togetherness:

1. Holidays
2. Religious obligations
3. Ethnic events
4. Anniversaries
5. Birthdays
6. Graduations
7. Funerals
8. Marriages
9. Births
10. Family illnesses

Invite the family over, especially on these occasions, and treat them well. You want his family to appreciate you and support you.

Learn from Widows

Widows can be a great help to your husband and you. They frequently comment, "Enjoy your life together— every day is a blessing," reminding you both that your time together is precious.

INTENSIFY CONVERSATIONS

Whether you're in love or angry at your husband, don't stop talking to each other. Invite communication just as you did when you were dating. Then, you said, "I could listen to you for hours," "Tell me more," or "How do you feel?" He needs clues that you want to listen, again. By conversation, we mean communication, the conveying and receiving of information and feelings.

You could benefit if your conversations have all four aspects of communication with your spouse. You are in a crisis, but you're not the first person whose spouse has wandered. You know that numerous women have faced your situation and many continued to be happily married. The right answer is what makes you happy. Use your conversation sparingly, since time has a value.

Interests in Common

Talk with your husband about your common interests, such as:

1. Emotions (likes, lusts, expectations)
2. Possessions and property
3. Thoughts different from yesterday's
4. Changes in your lives
5. New acquaintances

Create happiness by talking about positives in your life. Most of these would be starting points for you:

1. Relatives
2. People
3. Foods
4. Activities
5. Aspects of home life
6. Work-related events
7. Entertainment
8. Holidays
9. Vacation spots
10. Achievements

In addition to happiness, look for clues of unhappiness:

1. Work dissatisfaction
2. World problems
3. Financial condition
4. Failures
5. Peeves

Talk Freely

Encourage him to talk freely. If he answers your questions and it brings other thoughts to his mind, let him talk! He'll discuss what's on his mind—present circumstances, or memories that are important to him. You can know him better than anyone else does. Evaluate these dichotomies in your relationship:

1. Strengths/Weaknesses
2. Self-confidence/Doubts
3. Happiness/Sadness
4. Most significant people in his life/Who he's excluded from his list
5. New friends/New enemies

Change Topics

Look at the change in topics since you were first married. Exciting issues and challenges may be forgotten. You could be talking about mundane events such as the car needing more oil, the dog chewing a slipper, and the price of coffee. You are not helping your relationship if you watch television together and vicariously feel the lives of the characters.

When you listen to him he feels he matters to you. Paying attention to him with interest creates the ambiance that will later turn his attention to you.

Break the habit of not talking about yourselves. These are types of conversational questions you can use:

1. If you had to do it over again, would you have studied your speciality?
2. If you won the lottery, would you want a red sports car or a chauffeur-driven limo?
3. Would you prefer a safari in Africa or sunbathing in the Caribbean?
4. What's the last true bargain you remember getting?
5. What do you think we will be doing ten years from now?
6. What would it take to make your working conditions ideal?
7. What's the last really good movie we saw?
8. Would you have liked more children?
9. Should we join a health club or exercise group?
10. What's a good New Year's resolution for us to make?

Kick open the door to communication if you've closed it. You can bring up any topic. As an excuse, indicate that you saw it on a talk show or read it in a newspaper.

When you ask a question, give him a chance to answer fully. Your question is one sentence, but his answer may be worth pages.

Keep It Interesting

Idle chatter commonly causes a man to leave his wife. In distinguishing worthless chatter, the key is whether it is interesting to you or him. You should be asking yourself, "How does it affect our lives?"

Since words can change moods, incite great passions, or entertain, use these techniques:

1. Speak about the people, places, and events your husband knows, not about your family and friends he hasn't met. Otherwise, your discussion is as exciting as hearing about someone's vacation as he points on the road map, but all you see are the red and blue lines.

2. Don't expect your husband to know everything that is important to you. Explain why you are interested in a topic or what the relationship is between you and the people you talk about.

Most men care about sports and sports statistics. They assume that women are as interested in sports as they are, and so they talk about the games and sports heroes. Most women make similar mistakes. A woman will talk about her friends as if her husband really knows about them. If your husband doesn't know the people you are talking about, for him it's like a soap opera he's listening to for the first time. Keep conversations to interests in common. If you're changing subjects, give him an introduction to your topic and create the frame of reference. If he shows no visible sign of interest in what you're saying after three or four minutes change topics.

3. Time your conversations to see how long you actually talk or listen. If you're talking more than half the time, you're at a disadvantage, and should back off. If he talks too infrequently, get uneasy; he is too quiet. The surest way to know if your husband is enjoying the conversation is by his participation through questions or comments or eye contact. When you know what impact your words or topics have, then create the moods you want.

Talking about his achievements and the qualities that make him good at what he does keeps him enthusiastic about his work and about you. He wants to brag about his successes, and explain his failures.

The Silent Type

If he is too silent, spice your conversations with challenges. Give him a reason to argue. Ask him, "Are you sure you really caught that touchdown pass?" "Isn't your brother smarter than you?"

The Talker

If he talks too much, let him know you need quiet time. Keep him informed about what's happening in the news, then ask how he would solve world problems. Encourage him to think about situations beyond family and work. One-upmanship is crucial. He'll need quiet time to think out his answers if you ask intelligent questions.

Agreement

Love does not mean being in agreement. You will have different views. Your husband might have hidden agendas.

You won't discover his unexpressed goals until you talk with him. Disparate views are not personal attacks.

Even if you disagree on basic matters like dress and political ideas, don't change yourself. If he changed you might not like the results.

MYTHS OF MARRIAGE

The marriage contract says togetherness for "better or worse," but what is better for one spouse might be worse for the other. If either spouse feels too imposed upon, the togetherness starts eroding. Here are some myths that are responsible for such unhappiness.

"We Are One"

You and your husband are not identical. If you're happy, you expect your spouse should feel the same way. No matter how much you love him, you're annoyed if your spouse doesn't think and feel the same way you do. His reactions and yours differ. When Johnny spills his milk, you may moan, your husband may laugh. Your idea of a pet might be a Chihuahua named Chi-Chi; his may be a Great Dane named Thor. If you take your disagreements personally, resentment will replace love.

"I Didn't Marry Her Family"

Your mate expects you to treat him as his female relatives treated him. You expect your mate to behave as the men in your family behaved. Enjoy your mate's strengths, and don't rely on your family expectations. Your father may be a whiz in mechanics, and you may know more about engines than your husband does. So what? Maybe he's a fantastic salesman! You can't knit him a sweater like his grandma did, but you're more competent at the computer than she is.

"It's Our Money"

Love does not give you consent to use each others' funds freely. Money can bring you together only if you share the burden of meeting the bills and have guidelines over the disposable income. Once a spouse thinks the other enjoys an unfair advantage, there's discontent. Whoever feels imposed upon must feel comfortable enough to negotiate a solution.

"Love Conquers All"

Don't strive for perfection. After all, he's not perfect either. The closeness of marriage magnifies each other's bothersome behavior. Now you can complain, and so can he! If you don't speak up, the frustration eventually will destroy your happiness or erupt in an unexpected lashing out at your mate.

Mutual criticism and humor about your imperfections will help. Your parents loved you dearly and told you off, and so will your mate. Airing grievances builds a longer and stronger relationship.

"If You Loved Me, You Would Know What I Want"

Your mate has no idea what's on your mind unless you tell him. If you expect him to please you, he has to know your desires. Discuss your needs, what amuses you, and your idea of fun. If you want jewelry for your birthday, say so. Otherwise, he may give you a dishwasher, and you would have no cause to complain!

Don't expect him to be a mind reader. It will take many years before your mate knows you well enough to anticipate your desires. Even then, your desires change.

"A Man Has Sexual Savvy"

Even if a man has had many sexual partners, he still may not be a sex expert or know how to please you. Explain what you like. If he doesn't please you, it won't be long before you resent pleasing him.

"Love Holds a Marriage Together"

What holds a marriage together is making the marriage good for each other. It's overlooking the temporary pains or angers because there is a common goal.

"I'll Make Him into a Wonderful Husband"

If you accepted your spouse because you thought marriage would change him, then you were acting on expectations and not reality. Marriage is an "as is" proposition.

"He Wants an Independent Woman"

If you get better jobs and earn more money, you can take care of yourself. He's aware of your growing independence. Assure him you need him more every day. He fears that you'll meet exciting men who make him look inadequate, and that eventually he will stand in the way of your career. He wants a woman who is independent from the world, not from him. He wants to count on you as a co-insurer in life.

"Time Heals All Wounds"

Time alone doesn't solve your problems. Ignoring serious problems increases their intensity and your unhappiness. Face problems as soon as you can so the healing of the wound can begin.

REVIVING FIDELITY

No one stays the same, not even if he tries. Judging someone from a photograph and holding that image of him forever misleads about what he looks like today. Your husband is not the same person you met and married, but you think of him as he was when you first knew him. His changes are invisible, so you might have overlooked them.

You can't maintain the newness of your early relationship. Curiosity, first commitments, the excitement of meeting each other's family and friends are a one-time event. However, a small change in him would make you curious. If he suddenly preferred classical to country music, decided to walk a mile every day, changed his hairstyle, or wanted a new wardrobe, you would wonder why.

If you've not monitored your husband's thoughts for a while, you don't know what his new ideas are. Ask the same questions you asked years ago. You won't get the same answers. You'll discover that part of him has become a stranger to you, and that newness can be exciting.

You've changed, too. Your changes increase his curiosity about you and keep him amused and interested.

CONCLUSION

With the techniques you've learned, you'll be better prepared if your husband ever commits adultery or even thinks about it. Remember, every husband, including yours, is a potential adulterer. And it's up to you, and him, to make sure that adultery doesn't happen. You'll know the warning signs, and how to compensate for them. You will have options, but it's up to you to make these choices.

Let me know your thoughts and comments, and especially your experiences in coping with his adultery or the techniques you use to forestall or prevent his infidelity. I can't respond to every letter, but I will try.

Margaret Kent, Attorney
Law Offices of Margaret Kent
1121 Crandon Blvd.
Key Biscayne, Fl 33139